Days

AND
THEN
THERE
WERE
EIGHT

A.T.T.W.E.
$3.95

And

PAUL MOLLOY

As much as Paul Molloy would like people to notice him for his successful TV column or the awards he has won, everyone seems most impressed by the fact that he is the father of eight children.

While his family was growing, so was his repertoire of anecdotes and stories about children and his views on child rearing were being put to a severe test. In AND THEN THERE WERE EIGHT he relates some of those anecdotes, some of the inevitable problems, and much of the fun that has resulted in having six girls and two boys.

How do they do it? Do they have a lot of money, a large house, and servants? No, but they have other compensations—such as nine close friends apiece. Space is a luxury, so is silence. The funny thing is that when Molloy did have privacy and quiet in which to work ... he couldn't work because of the silence.

The greatest key to their smoothly-run household is discipline. Paul and his wife, Helen, firmly believe that discipline, not the lack of it, is a manifestation of parental love. They believe that a child bright enough to reject turnips in favor of cookies is almost bright enough to begin picking up after himself. Consequently each child

(continued on back flap)

And Then There Were

EIGHT

by Paul Molloy

DOUBLEDAY & COMPANY, INC.
GARDEN CITY, NEW YORK

Library of Congress Catalog Card Number 61–12558
Copyright © 1961 by Paul Molloy
All Rights Reserved
Printed in the United States of America

Prologue

I WANT to make it thoroughly clear that I'm proud of my children, if only because I'm stuck with the eight creatures and there isn't much of an alternative. But I'm also proud of my career, for the creativeness of writing a column every day is somewhat more demanding than the occasional act of procreativeness. So I'm always a little depressed when I'm introduced at functions as some sort of friendly stallion rather than a professional writer. It's a bit unnerving to find yourself pushed or pulled into a group by some well-meaning clod who announces, for the whole darn room to hear, "I want you people to meet Paul Molloy." (Pause.) "He has eight children, you know."

Not: "He's a newspaperman," or "He's an entertainment critic." Not a word about the paper. Just: "He has eight children, you know."

Well, where do you go from there? You feel a little naked during the pause that follows as they wait for you to say something. Oh, they're pleasant enough about it, but behind the smiling façades you begin to sense strange thoughts, such as, "Sex maniac. Written all over his face." (Some people read lips; I read eyes.)

This makes it difficult to get the conversation going, so after nodding wretchedly all around, you try to back away—preferably through the kitchen and out the back door. Then —and this *always* happens—someone in the group comes alive to shriek, "Eight children! You must be Catholic!"

5

Once this clumsy rapport has been established, the next question is usually, "Tell me—how do you do it?"

I've often been tempted to keep a frozen face and explain in detail precisely how fatherhood comes about, but so far I have resisted the temptation. I'm just chicken, I guess.

Frequently, well-meaning people I meet will ask to see pictures of the children, almost daring me to prove my breeding abilities. I don't carry pictures now, though I did until the sixth child arrived. Then my pocketbook got top-heavy and I found myself listing to starboard.

Anyway, this business of updating snapshots can become expensive when you have eight, because almost every month one of them is a year older. I find it hard to get excited when a father pulls snapshots from his pocket and says, "This is Marigold when she was three; she gets her Master's next month." Or: "Here's Humphrey as a Boy Scout; he made me a grandfather last week."

Beyond the cost and labor involved in pocket exhibits, there's the problem of whether people really care about looking at your snapshots. I proved it to myself once when I stuffed my pocketbook with eight poses of our firstborn, all taken when he was a month old. When an actress I was interviewing asked to see the tribe, I showed her the series and explained, "I like to remember them all as babies."

"What a charming idea," she trilled, barely glancing at them. "You can tell these three are girls, and look how the different personalities stand out!"

Sometimes, though, the conversation will eventually veer to such basic matters as how to go about the daily care of eight youngsters without yielding to total madness. Parents beat by the handling of two keep asking how we manage to cope with the sound of eight aloud and at once, and the fury of battle over box tops, and the smell of diapers, and the countless cuts and sprains, and the weeks when it's only hamburgers, and the little fears of childhood that are really big fears, and the nagging duty of punishment, and the mittens lost in the snow, and the memos from the dentist, and the first brassière, and the panic that you can't run from any of this, and the horrible guilt that comes from putting your wife in aproned slavery, and through it all the delicious little smiles and songs and wondrous blessings.

To remember the small things is to return to the big ones—Patricia's death (there were really nine), the flood that demolished the first house, the time we lost Georgia for twenty-four hours, the time we gave up our country for this one, in wonder and in fear, and the time we learned another baby was coming—and again that time, and again that time.

But for all the drama, there was on our crowded little stage a great deal of comedy kept on cue by a remarkable cast of characters with dispositions that prevented me from throwing in the towel. The cast:

> Helen, a beautiful lady with a sense of humor
> Paul, 14, a boy
> Georgia, 13, a girl
> Shonagh, 11, a girl
> Nelda, 8, a girl
> Marcia, 6, a girl
> Lisa, 4, a girl
> Barbara, 3, a girl
> Mark, 2, a boy

That's the way it went—one boy, then six girls in a row, and then another boy. And the last one came Christmas morning, during midnight mass.

As I say—my wife has a sense of humor.

And Then There Were EIGHT

Chapter 1

EACH year-end, the people around us seem to get the jitters over what we're going to do about Christmas, or what Christmas may do to us. When December comes, they don't wish us a Merry Christmas; it's more as if they were daring us, with a mixture of awe and ugh, to have one. "I bet," they'll bet, "it's going to be a real big Christmas at your house, with all those kids and all."

Well, of course it is. It's a big month, really, for the Christmas dream of children sets in early and the fulfillment lingers long after the wreath comes off the door. But then, all our Christmases are wild. The one I suppose I shall always remember in fear and fondness is the Christmas of 1958, when Helen was in the waning days of waiting for our latest. Mark was due around New Year's Day.

It has been a family custom that at the age of seven, the child becomes eligible for midnight mass. This was started by my father, and the remembrance of those reverent ventures into the raw, still night remains vivid to this day—our shadows in the snowbank nagging us to step up the pace . . . the resin smell of spruce cones from the outdoor crèche in the churchyard . . . the muffled, giggly greetings in the vestibule, and from within the wheezy bravado of the little organ bluffing through "*Minuit Chrétien*."

Besides the rare thrill of rising from bed in the crisp darkness of late night, the Christmas Eve service removed the obligation of mass on Christmas morning. Thus we were free to spread and stretch the delicious ecstasy of opening gifts. But, more important, it stamped in our minds the indelible doctrine that Christmas was, foremost, the birthday of the Christ Child. So strong was that impression in those growing years that conveying it to our own youngsters was a natural and simple thing. The true training of the child does not start at school or church; it begins at the knees of the mother.

So it was that Helen, ungainly now and cautious with weight, led Paul and Georgia and Shonagh into a front pew, and I tried to remember where on earth I'd hidden Nelda's top—the one with the ballerina pirouetting out of the burgeoning rose. Then the priest was in the pulpit, and we stood as he introduced the Gospel of St. Luke, and suddenly I remembered that the top was inside the tub hanging on the wall of the utility room, and out of the candled blur up front droned the voice of the priest:

". . . and it came to pass while they were there that the days for her to be delivered were fulfilled. And she brought forth . . ."

And at this instant I felt the sudden nudge of Helen's elbow on my arm and I turned to find in her eyes a brief flicker of fear. She glanced sideways. "I think," she whispered, "we'll have to go."

"Go?" I said, much too loud. There had been no warning that the baby was near. Well, not that near, anyway.

Helen leaned over. "I think it's time. We'd better go." And then she winced in a silent stab of pain. "Now!" she said.

Good God, I thought, recalling the sometimes suddenness of these things (Barbara had arrived four minutes after we entered the hospital). And as I gathered up the mittens and the boots and the scarves, I felt the cold clasp of panic—let no man tell you he gets used to these things—and for one ghastly moment a qualm buckled my knees. *The baby's coming now, right in this church, right by that manger.*

12

But we had time and there was no need to crowd into the manger. It was, however, a long, slow walk down the middle aisle and out of the church, and as we hustled into the tired little car—as much as you can hustle with a full pregnancy—Paul (then twelve) leaned over and said, "The thing to do, Dad, is not to get excited." Georgia and Shonagh assured me that everything would be all right because as we were walking out they had said some "real hard" prayers.

Here it was, only hours to the monumental explosion of Christmas, and the minds of the little ones were pausing on prayer and calm and the comfort of their mother. There's anxiety in the daily struggle, but there are rewards.

We scudded home and of course there could be no *réveillon* (hot broth, cookies, milk) for the young midnight massers this time. The baby sitter agreed to stay through the night, and I drove to the hospital, thinking, It's Christmas, and we've been expecting a fat little stranger with rosy cheeks and twinkling eyes, but this is ridiculous.

It was a long, laborious birth, and it was 5 A.M. before I reached home again for what would have ordinarily been the most important chore of the day: the laying out of gifts beneath the tree. Part of our Christmas custom is to trim the tree two days before Christmas, but there is no gift in sight until the children dart out of their beds on Christmas morning to gape at the order and mystery of the colorful array beneath the tree. Even then, no gift is opened until breakfast is over and the dishes have been cleared, for there's enough tinseled tumult later on without the chaos of a cluttered kitchen. It's a pained wait for the little ones, but I remember it as a pain that feels good.

I placed the last gift beneath the tree at ten minutes to seven, poured a cup of coffee, and awaited the delayed-action shock of Mark's startling arrival. At five minutes to seven the first Christmas scream wahooed from one of the bedrooms, the mob bounded into the living room, and the far-

13

rago was on. Before it got out of hand I lined them up, called for silence, and announced, with as much sangfroid as I could muster, "Mommy had a very nice baby during the night. Now you all have a little brother."

I had to explain to the younger ones why Mark and his mother wouldn't be home for Christmas. With that out of the way, Paul, who had had six sisters in succession, said, "Gee . . . He can have my clothes and my baseball stuff." It's strange what avenue a young mind will take under emotion.

"Let's call him Jesus," said Nelda, "like the little Jesus."

"No, we'll call him Mark," I said.

"I think Jesus is gooder," said Nelda.

"No, it's not," Shonagh chided, making everything all right. "The kids at school will call him Jeez for short."

(It happens that Helen and I dislike nicknames, and the children have been taught not to use them. They know they are not to address Barbara as Barb or Babs, and Lisa is not to become Liz.)

At this point Georgia, who gets frightfully motherly at times, told the tribe to shush up. "We're going to kneel now," she ordered, "and say a prayer." And we did.

I feel a little awkward about the pride involved in relating this, but I'm reporting it precisely as it happened.

(On the subject of reports—I received a phone call later in the day from a friend in the television business. I told him about the oddity of our Christmas, and he evidently passed it along to others, for the next day it appeared in the morning paper as a gay holiday item. It was touching, except for one thing: it appeared in the opposition paper. Within twenty-four hours of his arrival, Mark had already made his mark by getting his old man's paper lightly scooped.)

When it was all over and I had come to Helen's bedside, the first thing she mumbled was, "He's beautiful . . . what are you going to do about the turkey?"

14

Now it was 10 A.M., and what in blazes *could* I do about it?

Because Helen has such a vast clientele she always gets a huge turkey, and that morning the creature looked like an adolescent pterodactyl. Luckily, it had been stuffed the day before. It was ready.

But was I?

What about that coat of aluminum foil, for example? Should I remove it now, or after the oven ordeal? And Helen's instructions—was I to set the oven at 350 degrees, or 530? And was it fifteen minutes for each pound, or fifty minutes? And what about that bawdy threading job on the derrière? Shouldn't I snip the stitches before the heat got at them? But if I snipped now, wouldn't the stuffing erupt all over the place? I felt terribly alone.

There was only one thing to do. I called the lady next door. "Helen had a turkey during the night," I stammered, "and I'm ready to put the baby in the oven, but I'm a little worried about . . ."

Before running over, the neighbor thoughtfully dispatched an alert to the neighborhood and within minutes a hastily assembled rescue party was streaming in through the front and back doors. They came with skillets and frozen peas and cookbooks and celery and large pans and small pots and cranberry jelly and gravy bowls and bags of potatoes, and some brought their children, but, most of all, they came with good intentions. One of them contributed a bottle and a carving set. "There's two things a man needs at a time like this," he rasped. "That's a strong snort and a sharp knife." He was so right.

Soon the kitchen was a sort of organized shambles, and I don't believe I've ever seen as much salad tossed—and missed —at one time as I did that forenoon. Everyone bustled about at some appointed task; others with afterthoughts kept running home for more provisions; and finally everything fell into place, the turkey was fine (you *don't* snip the stitches until it's done), and there were so many cans and jars left over that when Helen came home five days later I still hadn't been to the grocery store.

Before she returned, though, I had a solid chance to appreciate the patience, know-how, and all-around guts it takes to be a homemaker. I'll probably lose the husbands right here, but it's time one of the clubs blew the whistle on the mealy-mouthed misdevotion with which much of the membership has wrapped itself. There's a cunning sanctimony surrounding married males by which they tend to hoist themselves to a pedestal. I have no objection to men occupying pedestals. It's just that I don't think they should shove off their wives.

It's almost impossible these days to leaf through a magazine without colliding into an essay directing wives to pamper and coddle and flatter and serve and adore their mates, for fear they may race—with fraudulent alibis flying—into the arms of other women. I'm a little weary of the cockeyed psychiatry that says the breadwinner is a delicate deity needing wall-to-wall reverence lest he drop dead from the strain of making a living.

I've become leery of the voice-of-doom pronouncements from self-appointed experts who tut-tut the woman for "upsetting" her husband with problems of the house and children. The fact that the house is his home and its occupants his kin seems to escape the off-balance logic of these counselors—some of whom are childless, or thrice-married, or both.

I don't intend to go to pieces over this, but it's a fraud that needs exposure. The gloomy-gus theory that women are nudging their husbands into an early grave leads many men into the neurotic haze of self-pity which often blinds them to the burdens of others. It turns them into sissified clods who take to their beds at the threat of a runny nose; into oafs who curse the eight-hour job and ignore the fourteen hours their wives put in on theirs; into dolts who never take

their wives to dinner, vegetate five nights a week on television, then regain their strength with a weekend of golf or
waist-deep in some swamp, assassinating ducks.

Housewives are constantly nagged into "understanding"
their husbands, soothing the tired brows of the poor dears.
To a point, fine. But I think a turnabout on this nonsense
is in order. I feel husbands owe it to themselves to try
"understanding" their wives for a change, and the only
way to do it properly is to take her place for a while, and
dig in.

Many husbands actually believe that the housewife's day
consists of clearing the breakfast dishes, making the beds,
and dusting—all of this in sexy high heels and to the second
movement from the Lestoil Symphony—followed by lunch,
a nap, and the preparation of dinner.

Nonsense.

At least once a year they might send their wives on a
seven-day vacation and take over the routine. Or, when
their wives are hospitalized, they might skip the house-
keeper, stay home from the office, and take over the helm.

I know what I'm talking about. I've done it several times.
While Helen was away recently, I tucked a towel around my
waist (I can't stand aprons on males), and mothered our
brood of eight for two weeks.

I'd prefer to forget the whole insane mess, but here's how
one of my days went—I made notes—as a homemaker.

I started at 6:30 A.M. with school lunches for Paul,
Georgia, Shonagh, and Nelda. It would have been simple
enough to send them to classes with a jelly sandwich, but I
figured I'd been turning out some pretty sad breakfasts and
the least I could do was make them a decent lunch. Then I
put on the coffee and studied the bad news out the window:
a snowstorm had made the roads too icy for Paul to pedal his
paper route. So after glancing at my column that morning

17

I had to get into the car and deliver it around the neighborhood.

After that, preparing breakfast for the crowd took almost an hour, during which I felt like a one-armed cook at a logging camp. There were such agonizing decisions to reach: should I butter the toast before it got cold, or should I give Mark his bottle? But if I did that, the porridge would boil over, and why was Barbara still in the nude in her high chair, and what did Nelda mean when she demanded two eggs—one fried and one poached?

Nagging the four eldest to the school bus and cleaning up took another hour (did you ever scrape baby food out of a toaster?). I had hoped to find a minute to shave, but there was a diaper to change, the milk to bring in, the dishes to wash, a diaper to change, Mark to bathe, the beds to make, a diaper to change, a washing to do, the furniture to dust, the phone to answer, the garbage to empty, a diaper to change, noses to wipe, two fights to settle, pajamas to hang up, a diaper to change—and to this day I don't know how those four coloring crayons got inside the bottle of prune juice.

I made it, though, just in time to haul everything out again and prepare lunch. Years of practice have taught me to open cans without slicing an artery, so the soup-and-sandwich routine was fairly smooth, except for an interruption at the door by some survey nut with a pad who wanted to know if I had detergent hands. All that lady got from me was a display of bad temper.

After their nap, during which I was able to write next day's column, I bundled up Marcia and Lisa (that took twenty minutes) for a romp in the snow. Precisely two minutes later they were at the door with a mad desire for the bathroom. By the time I got through the unbundling and rebundling, the four others had returned from school and it was time to go to the village for groceries. In the advertisements, the visit to the supermarket is a journey of exotic

18

enchantment, but I had to hold Mark in one arm, guide the cart with the other (all the while balancing Barbara on the cart's baby seat), and keep track of the six others, who insisted on filling up the basket with body-building items such as hot dogs, marshmallows, and Coke. I did find a new, delightful timesaver, though: ready-cooked potatoes that come in a can.

There were some disastrous interludes—when we rolled home I found I had a flat. After slipping on the spare, I found it was flat too (this really happened). To save garbage space I stomped a supposedly empty egg carton, but it still contained an egg. Lisa locked herself in the bathroom, and I had to remove the storm window in deep snow. Not only that, a Hollywood press agent chose that very moment to ring me long-distance. I neglected to wash colored clothes separately, and now we have pink bedsheets and two of my hankies are a sort of purple-chartreuse. I was never able to mate the children's socks properly after they came out of the dryer, and did you ever try to screw a storm window back into place on a dark, wintry night? There were also broken toys, skinned knees, and lost mittens, but these were minor problems.

It was time to set the table for dinner, and I was drained. If I'd been a woman and my husband had barged in at that point with, "Hi, honey, I'm home," I could only have stared out the window and muttered, "Big deal."

I looked at the chops in the freezer, but I couldn't bring myself to the task. So for dinner that night we had hot dogs, marshmallows, and Coke.

And ready-cooked potatoes that come in a can.

Then came the ritual of the homework, the ritual of the bath, the ritual of bedtime stories, the ritual of prayers, and the ritual of tuck-in-my-covers-and-you-kissed-me-but-I-didn't-kiss-you.

My day had begun at 6:30 A.M. At 10:30 P.M. I sat down for the first time, lit a cigarette and picked up a magazine. There it was, on page 12, in big, black letters: "IS TODAY'S MOTHER GETTING TOO SOFT?"

Chapter 2

I DEARLY hope no one will feel I have an obsession about bathrooms, but at our house the bathroom is a chamber of wholesale importance. And not necessarily because of its primary function.

I mean, there are ten of us at home, and it doesn't take crack logistics to picture the near chaos of who gets the bathroom when and for how long. This is perhaps as close as I'll get to conceding severe hardship in large families.

I don't know how it all started, but our bathroom becomes a sort of social center for the youngsters in the morning. The electric buzz of the razor seems to be a clarion call that summons them from all over to exchange pleasantries (and unpleasantries), to sing, wrestle, and ask—for the umpty-umpth time—what in the world is that hair doing in my armpits?

I know what you're thinking: Why doesn't the idiot lock himself in?

Well, it happens I'm a no-breakfast man. I go from bed to bathroom to business, pausing on my way out only to scald my throat with coffee. There is, therefore, no morning muster for me at the breakfast table. We do our collective bargaining at the dinner hour.

I don't feel this is enough time for the little ones to speak their pieces, especially since I often have a few pieces of my own to speak at sundown. Further, there are too many nights when I can't make it to dinner.

So the sunup ablution has developed into a moment of

communion when the children perch on the edge of the bathtub to how and why and where and when and what me into wakefulness: How do the angels fly? (well, how do they?), and why does Mommy have a bump on her tummy again? (so often I've wondered), and where does the man go when you turn off the television? (I don't know but I have a suggestion), and when does Easter come again? (good grief, it was here only last week), and what was that word I said when Lisa spilled the Kool-Aid on the typewriter (I didn't say anything. I just rammed my head against the wall).

And invariably the most important question, the one requiring an immediate answer, comes when your mouth is a) full of gargle or b) screwed every which way to accommodate the razor.

Then Paul saunters in for approval on his homework and while I'm groping for a towel I get involved in a ridiculous debate over the Revolutionary War, because in Canada I studied history from the British side—Cornwallis was the good guy—and how do you tell your son you consider Ethan Allen an unmitigated rogue? Then Georgia demands that I button her pinafore, and Shonagh suddenly recalls I forgot last week's allowance (did you ever dig down deep to discover you're still in your shorts?), and Nelda wants to know where her left shoe is (it's always the left one that wanders off), and Marcia reminds one and all that this is Puffed Wheat morning, for she hates porridge (which is Friday's fare), but Lisa shouts for Sugar-Crisp because the current cutouts have a blue frock her collection lacks, and Barbara whimpers that I've forgotten her ritual—a soupçon of aftershave behind each ear—and from Mark's crib comes the testy garble that translates into "Why-the-heck-haven't-I-been-changed-yet?"

And this is the point where Helen warns that it's twelve minutes to train time, and you shudder at the madness of it all, because it was this way yesterday and it will be tomorrow and all of the days. And just when agony grips at the guts, the tribe will interrupt the battle of the box tops and one will pipe, "Daddy, can't you stay home with us today?"

So the ceremonial kiss-as-kiss-can (nine kisses) is dispatched like a stone skimming a pond and you go out into the world, face stained with baby food (strained apricot), lipstick, marmalade, and plain old saliva. And the smell of it is strange for a little while, but the taste of it reaches to the heart, and it's like all the possessions of the world, and twice that.

This is why I savor the importance of our matutinal assemblies, even if the locale is cramped. Come to think of it, our bathroom is crowded if you're in there alone because it's such a convenient catchall. There's the round-bellied diaper pail that sounds like sixty cymbals when you stumble on it in the dark of night. There's the portable potty seat for the amateurs—someday these will be gone and I'll know middle age is here—and there's the bathroom scale, which never ceases to fascinate. For several weeks Marcia thought it was a clock.

And toothbrushes—we must have a hundred toothbrushes. Well, maybe not that many, but enough to scrub the deck of a carrier. It seems that each time I slide open the door of the medicine cabinet, out falls another one. For all I know, maybe they mate in there.

But there's more—Helen's stocking dangling to dry and Georgia's leotards and Shonagh's slips and Nelda's socks, the changing array of pajama bottoms, and shower caps, an occasional wet sheet, and sometimes a doll or stuffed cat banished to the porcelain prison for some misdemeanor. Some days it doesn't pay to look for a towel.

With only one tub and a limited hot-water supply—we owe a lot to Lake Michigan—staggered baths are imperative. After the tub has been relieved of rubber ducks, plastic ships (our fleet tops that of Switzerland), and sponge barracuda, the line-up looks like this: Mark has a daily forenoon priority,

I shower in the morning, and Helen takes her chances when the brood is abed; Paul gets Sundays and Wednesdays; Georgia has Mondays and Thursdays; Shonagh takes Tuesdays and Fridays; Nelda soaks Wednesdays and Sundays; Marcia dips Thursdays and Mondays; Lisa gets Fridays and Tuesdays, and Barbara plunges in between Paul and Nelda on Wednesdays and Sundays.

Saturday night is set aside for scouring the rings out of the tub.

So in many ways we have the ultimate in togetherness, but it has its good points. We have, for instance, no mice. An occasional ant, yes. But any mouse that would dare intrude into this stunted chalet would wind up hunchbacked in twenty-four hours. More important, however, a togetherness like this has to be a constant adhesive.

Of course bodies keep bumping together in the hall, but with all the inconvenience, we keep bumping souls too. And plainly there isn't enough of that in the family today. If parents and children bumped into each other more often, they'd be less inclined to drop one another later on.

Stroll down your street someday, and count off the stepchildren. . . .

There's no denying the nuisance of crowding, but it's an oddity of human nature that we can adjust to nuisance more smoothly than, say, to sudden wealth. Take our car, for instance (and I rather wish you would; it's eight years old).

Back in 1953 I managed with the help of a finance company to acquire a two-door sedan which, in those days, seemed like a large, luxurious chunk of sleek steel. We had only four children then.

Today it looms little larger than the runty compacts that have taken over the streets, especially when ten of us squeeze in for a run to the market.

But I will say it has served us well, and somewhere I detect the gentle hand of Providence (Detroit Division), for in those eight years it has seldom let us down. It isn't pretty any more, and the glow is gone from its cheeks, but I never cease to admire its endurance. On impossibly cold wintry mornings I have watched the new chariots of our neighbors belch frustrating fumes all over the area, then cough into wretched immobility. And for some reason that defies explanation, carburetors, and all that jazz, our humble little clunk has purred gaily through the most ghastly vagaries of climate. Maybe it's sorry for us.

Be that as it may, we must make an outlandish picture when the clan rolls into the village square (Hinsdale, pop.: 13,400) and debarks for the processional down the main avenue.

I have seen unnerved citizens cluster on corners to stare and point and frown as, first, I emerge to help Helen with Mark in her arms, followed by Paul who helps Georgia (sometimes), followed by Shonagh who helps Nelda, followed by Marcia, Lisa, and Barbara, who prefer to bounce out unaided, thank you. We must look like that ancient circus stunt wherein dozens of clowns flounce out of a midget auto.

With ten in the car, I suspect we're breaking the law, but the cop on the corner must be a sympathetic soul, for he always looks the other way. Either that or he can't stand the sight of it.

Because room space is a far-out luxury which we'll likely never attain, watching television as a group presents its problems. Not long ago I had to review a new children's show, an appalling mediocrity hosted by one of those middle-aged male performers who feel that the way to get their message across to children is to slaughter the English language.

The mob assembled at my curtain call, including Mark, who bellied in clutching the electronic channel selector. Since discovering the click-off blessings of the selector, Mark hasn't let it out of his grasp. He finds in it the security that other kids find in a blanket.

25

Such a caucus at our house calls for planning, in this case Plan A-II (Plan A-I is for eating arrangements when company drops in). The sofa went into the hall; Nelda, Marcia, and Lisa mounted the bleachers (bookshelf); and down came the south wall (which opens into a room where I keep my desk). We were still crowded, so Helen—as is usual in these cases—withdrew to the carport and we spread lunch on the floor.

"Ain't dis fun!" cried the host, who seemed in deathly fear of lisping. Mark reacted by promptly clicking him off the screen.

"Let's watch Small World," whined Lisa, who's a bit of an intellectual. The star bounced back with the first of four pie-in-the-face routines.

"He don't got good manners," Marcia chided.

"He can't duck," snapped Georgia.

Nelda scrambled down from the bleachers. "I've got homework," she said in apparent relief.

"Dis dessert is de tops!" bellowed the host, smacking his lips.

"We haven't said grace yet," said Shonagh, removing Barbara's foot from the butter. Now on his third pie, the star screamed, "Kids, tell your mudder dis is National Try-Custard-for-Breakfast Week!"

The thought of whipping up a batch of that dessert at 6:15 in the morning, and us just barely over National Try-Peanut-Butter-after-School Week, was enough to make a grown man cry. And I did. Mark, a sympathetic sort, handed me his selector and gestured that I should hold it to my cheek. Soon I was able to pull myself together, but then Barbara gathered stray crumbs off the floor, plus the second page of my notes, and nimbly gobbled the whole bit.

How do you like the show so far?" I asked, retrieving my pencil from the mayonnaise jar.

Paul gazed out the window. "Can I stay up for the late

show tonight if I mow the lawn?" he asked, eying the season's first snowfall. Lisa announced from the distance that she was going outside. Barbara rolled over in the potato chips and promptly fell asleep. Marcia and Lisa got into an argument about how many days to Christmas (Lisa's final verdict: "Soon in some little tomorrows") and wandered off.

Paul tried again. "Sure, the late show is just a Western," he said hopefully, "but there's a lot of history in it and you learn things that way." Shonagh and Georgia brought their mother back inside and to the furnace room to thaw out. "We'll rearrange the furniture now," she said gently. The star trilled good-by with, "Wasn't dis fun?" Mark blinked at the screen, wiped a little drool off his chin, and sadly punched his selector.

And I had myself a column for the day.

Let them laugh at togetherness. There's much to be said for it.

Chapter 3

HELEN had to have a sense of humor to marry me in the first place.

To begin with, we met on a blind date, and my very first sight of her was a pair of legs reflected in a hotel-room mirror. I practically fell apart before that vision. Further, while our courtship lasted about a year, I saw her but twice in all that time and kissed her only once. And it wasn't much of a kiss, either; it was one of those embarrassed pecks on the forehead, on a busy Montreal street. The second time I kissed her was in church, twenty minutes after we had become man and wife. But it was a real kiss, that one.

(Any woman will understand that this incident isn't Helen's favorite story. But a lot of people already know of it, so I'm not compounding the sacrilege by telling it here. A year after we came to the United States, I sold a story to the *Saturday Evening Post*, and since I was a "new author" the magazine ran a biographical sketch at the back of the book which included the story of our strange courtship. When Helen saw the nice family picture used by the *Post*, I think she finally forgave me for being such a lousy lover.)

While our mothers had known each other, Helen and I had moved in different circles as teen-agers in the Canadian city of Winnipeg. She had gone from convent life to that of a debutante. I had gone from the University of Manitoba to the bottom of a Quebec copper mine, and thence to newspaper work in Montreal. I was twenty-four and a reporter when we met, and not too keen on girls; I wanted to become a writer, and, besides, playboys don't thrive on thirty dollars a week.

One day in 1944 Helen came to Montreal on a visit with her mother, and my sister, Denise, who had known the family, thought it would be nice if I took Helen out on the one night she would be in the big city. I had an assignment that night, but I decided to go to the hotel and pay my respects to my family's friends.

When Helen's mother opened the door, the first thing I saw was that pair of brown legs in a mirror at the end of the room; they were crossed seductively, much as is done in today's TV commercials. I followed her mother into the room (I think I really ran in ahead of her) and found Helen sitting on the bed, applying leg tan, which was quite the thing in those days.

I fell in love with those limbs then and there. They were long and of delicate sinew, and the calves had the sort of curves that make men grit their teeth. To this day they retain the luscious shape they had that night—a slinky tribute to the exercise that comes from picking up after eight children. Her eyes were about the size of half-dollars, and I was stricken by those too.

While only a reporter at the time, I was getting evening assignments to cover night clubs and the last gasps of vaudeville, and my job that night was to interview an up-and-coming stripteaser who was causing some commotion in Montreal—church and police commotion. On an impulse, I invited Helen to come along with me, and she was elated at the prospect of seeing her first vaudeville show. My only concern was to see her home quickly after the performance, then get to the office to write my story.

Midway during the atrocious program a comic magician picked on Helen—we were in the first row—and cajoled her into coming onstage to help him with his stunts. I suggested that she stay put, but she wanted to be a good sport about

29

it. As happens in the low comedy of vaudeville, the performer's chitchat and tricks were in rather poor taste. (The climax of his act was to tug at the back of her dress and come up with a pair of trick panties concealed in his sleeve.) I remember standing in the wings, dying a little with each stunt, and wishing I could ring down the curtain. I didn't think she would ever wish to speak to me again, but a lady remains a lady—no matter what the surroundings.

As if I hadn't had enough embarrassment for one night, I happened to be standing in the wrong place when the stripper went into her act a few minutes later. Nearing the close of her "exotic dance," she loftily flung her brassière into the wings, and it hit me right in the face. Not that this is a catastrophe; but on a man's first date it did seem a little inappropriate.

Immediately after her performance, we followed her into her dressing room for the interview. It was a bit crowded with the three of us in this hole in the wall, but what made it shocking was that the dancer neglected to don a gown while we were with her, and I remember that when I got back to the office I wasn't able to decipher my notes too well. At the end of our chat, during which Helen, some distance from the convent now, blushed out loud, the stripper turned to her and asked, "And what did you think of my act?" It seemed an inane thing for this particular type of artist to ask of a woman, but Helen smiled gently and said, "I must say, it's quite an act." I thought this critique was a high mark in diplomacy.

Several months later Helen came to Montreal on another visit, and this time my sister didn't have to coax me. I thought we would spend the evening in one of the city's nicer clubs, but Helen, who came from a well-to-do family, didn't seem exactly thrilled with the idea of sitting around a table and dancing. Since a reporter has entree into unusual places, she wondered if I might show her the "other side" of the big town. (That first date might not have been a smash, but it apparently hadn't been a total flop.)

As a starter, I took her to one of Montreal's notorious dens, where she watched girls casually slug their escorts with a bottle for rubbernecking. It was there she discovered a then-popular drink among local habitués—a swallow of straight whisky washed down with a half-and-half. A half-and-half consisted of one part beer, one part tomato juice, and a raw oyster, presumably so worrywarts could build themselves up while tearing themselves down. Helen had one half-and-half and since then has touched neither beer, tomato juice, nor oysters.

The next stop was the central police station which, on a late Saturday night, is generally jumping. I had friends there, on this side of the big tank, and with a keen sense of professional pride they displayed the current assortment of flotsam swept in from the streets.

I have seen hopelessly deranged men locked up, but somehow the skid-row unfortunates in the big tank have always been a sadder sight to me.

Helen turned her head and touched her eyes. "I just never thought that life could be so awful," was all she said.

The sergeant must have thought the party was lagging, for he said to Helen, "Does Mademoiselle now wish to see *les putains* [the prostitutes]?"

"Some other time," I said.

Directly across the street was the morgue, and I took Helen there because one of the attendants was both a friend and a character. He was an expert on the city's underworld activities, and an authority on crimes of violence. I had begun to write detective stories on the side at the time, and he had often helped me. He told Helen a few hair-raising stories and, before we left, insisted on showing her the refrigerated room where the corpses were kept. Two of them were children, and I thought Helen would flinch, but she was sturdier about it than I was.

I kept worrying about what her mother would say if we told her where we had been.

Into the cool, quiet night again we walked the two miles to Helen's hotel. What we had seen and heard that night had gently nudged the reserve, the unknown, between us. Had we gone dancing, we might have come home talking about the band and the night view of the city from on high. Now we talked of life and death and people, and in so doing, we touched each other's souls at once. We were strangers no more.

We couldn't have been, because my proposal followed a few minutes later. As we neared the hotel she slipped her arm into mine, and I remember thinking that this must be the sign of love. It's strange how you remember a commonplace gesture like that.

But the important thing—why I asked her to marry me at just this point—I can't remember.

Perhaps I was weary of long-distance courting by letter and telephone (one phone call, one especially reckless night, had cost me $52.50).

Perhaps it was the sudden, crude encounter with loneliness, for we had been with terribly lonely people. And we ourselves, I know now, were lonely that night.

Perhaps it was the discovery that Helen had taken the entire evening without giggling or gagging. I had seen and felt the compassion.

Perhaps it was those legs.

Whatever it was, she said yes. And I kissed her on the forehead.

And then I went home.

Chapter 4

THERE is wry humor in the plight of the poor fellow who cripples himself in the early hours of his honeymoon. Almost everyone has a friend or relative who turned an ankle tripping into the bridal suite, or wrenched a shoulder tugging at luggage in the upper berth. Those who don't, often invent one. I have an honest-to-kinfolk cousin who was carted off to the hospital during his wedding breakfast with a burst appendix. What gave his condition some flavor was that he was a hospital administrator; he spent his honeymoon a few doors from his office, immobile and lonely.

From puberty onward I have had only two colds, but both were unforgettable. The first one came in my teens, sending me to the hospital for three months with rheumatic fever. The other came on the eve of the wedding.

I had come a thousand miles from the east to Winnipeg to assert, publicly and before an altar, that I believed in the rule that no man should lay his put-asunder hands on what God had joined. The journey, the ordeal of bicycling around town to meet Helen's populous relatives, and the built-in tension of the wedding itself led to my second, explosive cold.

Because it was a serious one—I snuffed out a nearby candle with a monumental sneeze that almost blew the ring out of the best man's hand—we decided to spend the first night in town. Besides, staying put seemed preferable to the bustle of travel on the night of the wedding day, giving us a chance to catch our newlywed second wind in solitude.

It developed, however, that a close friend suddenly felt overwhelming concern that we might become bored in our hotel room. He volunteered to drop by to enliven our first hours as man and wife. It was difficult to reject his intentions, ill timed though they were, on two counts: our college friendship had been a cordial one; and he had been kind enough to photograph the ceremony. Unfortunately, he failed to keep his mission a secret, mentioning it to his brother, who in turn told his friends, who in turn told their friends. As I look back on it now, the word must have passed along to anyone who cared to listen.

What was to have been a short visit from a college pal quickly deteriorated into the sort of shambles that often attends the groom the night *before* his wedding. By nine o'clock there must have been twenty people in our room, including three or four I'd never seen before who kept muttering that it was difficult to toast the newlyweds without something to toast with. Therefore I had to send for drinks at frightening and costly intervals.

Adding to the confusion, some of those discreet enough to stay away from the hotel now felt inspired to elaborate on greetings they had dispensed all morning. Every twenty minutes or so a bellhop would appear at the door with clever telegrams like: "So you thought you fooled us. Ha-ha. Much love," or, "Did you leave a call for morning? Ha-ha. Much love."

Soon the place was in an uproar. Telegrams and flowers and an occasional stranger kept drifting in; two of the crashers telephoned their friends to come on over; I was sick enough to wonder if I'd be laid out in my wedding suit; and what was left of Helen's corsage couldn't have been pressed into a bankbook. It's a tribute to her tolerance that she maintained her calm even when a stranger edged us into a corner, raised his glass, and said, "You make a nice couple, kids. Happy days."

34

"Thanks," I said, "but I didn't catch your name."

"Kems," he said. "Joe Kems. Don't you remember? I'm your bellhop."

"Oh," I said. "Nice of you to stop in."

When the last intruder had stepped out the door, we were left with a cluttered room rancid with the smell of dried pickles, soggy cigarette butts, and stale drinks. On her very first night as a housewife, Helen spent thirty minutes collecting garbage.

Now it was three o'clock in the morning, and we spent the rest of the night at the window, watching the dawn drift over the serene, sleeping city. Because of my bellowing cough, Helen insisted I wrap myself in a blanket, and as we stood at the window I thought of how ridiculous I looked, and of my cousin incapacitated by his appendix, and of the only real kiss I had given Helen, and none of it seemed funny any more. Yet we would always remember the first night of married life.

For the very first time we had seen the soundless flash of a sunrise.

By the time we got married I had left the newspaper in Montreal to join a news agency which sent me to manage its French-Canadian bureau in Quebec City. It was there we made our first home together, but I had a devil of a time setting it up. Finding a decent apartment toward the end of the war was almost impossible. There seemed only to be single rooms, which the French-Canadians insisted on calling "apartements," because they were equipped with a sofa-bed and a hot plate. For weeks before the wedding I tramped the streets in the early hours before work and in the evenings, knocking on doors until my knuckles looked like small rainbows. As soon as the papers came out I would scan the want ads, but there was no getting through on the telephone:

hundreds of other couples had the same problem, and the frustration of busy signals was everywhere.

Many a night I would pocket the ads and prowl about the city by bus. But this was a slow, laborious process, and invariably I was too late, and the only consolation was that perhaps those who had beaten me there had a more urgent need than mine. I even took to whizzing to some addresses by cab, only to find on arrival that the room had been snapped up, sight unseen, by telegram.

Finally I realized that I would have to resort to some form of hanky-panky: I would have to see those ads before they appeared in the paper. On the face of it, this may have been slightly dishonest, but I excused it with the reminder that I was after all, in the news business (besides, there was something fishy about the way I kept losing out to telegrams).

A friend employed on a newspaper agreed to skulk around the ad department and scan the ads before they were to appear in print. On the fourth day of this subterfuge he relayed a find which, for rent and locale, seemed appropriate.

When I presented myself at the door, I was met by a lady of ample bosom and ample voice (whisky baritone) who informed me that I was welcome to the "apartement," provided I bought the key—for fifty dollars. Then, as now, fifty dollars was a lot of money, but the concierge, a Mme. Labossière, made it plain that wherever I went I would find the key racket a postwar reality. The fifty dollars, plus the month's advance rent which Mme. Labossière required, was more than I had in the bank. But she agreed to take a postdated check.

It's all rather depressing to look back on it now, but besides the inevitable sofa-bed and hot plate, the place contained a rickety kitchen table and two chairs, a nineteenth-century dresser, a paper-thin throw rug, and the must of decades. It didn't even have a clothes closet—coat hangers hung on hooks nailed into the wall—and the only mirror was in the communal bathroom down the hall.

It also had a tiny porch hanging from the window, which Mme. Labossière grandly identified as a *"balcon,"* which, she croaked, would be ideal to refrigerate the food. It was to a balcony what a boulder is to Grand Canyon.

And the nook had cockroaches.

Mme. Labossière's flat squatted atop a printing shop in an ancient, two-story structure. The heat from the plant below was oppressive, and every few seconds there arose the *sssttt-plonk!* din of the printing press downstairs.

The three other rooms were occupied by two women in their early thirties and a sullen, silent man who worked nights in a coal yard. He would return from his job in the morning literally black with coal dust, which he would immediately wash off in the bathroom. Each morning Helen would have to scrub the hideous black stains he had left in the tub and sink before she could attend to her own ablutions.

This tenant's slovenly habits were one unpleasantness. Another took a little time before becoming apparent.

Mme. Labossière, fortyish and deserted (she claimed) by a *"maudit chien"* of a husband, lived alone in premises at the end of the hall. Despite a mild touch of dissipation, her face showed traces of former beauty. I saw more evidence shortly after we moved in when I went to her apartment to complain about the cockroaches.

Hanging from the wall were more than a dozen photographs of herself in the nude. Each was posed in what might be called an artistic mood, and she wasn't in the least backward in showing off the gallery and asking for comment?

"I guess you were a"—*sssttt-plonk!*—"model once?" I asked, the printing press downstairs punctuating my panic.

"Oh, no," she said. "These are just"—*sssttt-plonk!*—"ordinary pictures. Do you think I look nice?"

"I think it's very"—*sssttt-plonk*—"interesting," I said. "Now about the cockroaches——"

"You will notice I still have the"—*sssttt-plonk!*—"figure," she went on, edging nearer. The back of my neck turned cold.

Mme. Labossière, who always wore a sort of white turban and liked to pad around barefoot, had strange tastes. There were bearskins all over the floor, and a couple more were slung over a couch in the corner. In addition, she had little incense pots going full blast around the room, which was in semidarkness at midafternoon. I could understand the nude poses, the crazy turban, and even the bearskins, but the incense floored me. A Freudian student would have had himself a whale of a study in that niche.

"Would you not say," persisted Mme. Labossière in that husky pule of hers, "that my"—*sssttt-plonk!*—"figure has not changed?"

"Yes, I would"—*sssttt-plonk!*—"not," I said, getting terribly mixed up.

By now Mme. Labossière had casually placed her hand in mine. "You will come back to"—*sssttt-plonk!*—"look at my pictures again, no?"

"No—uh, yes," I stammered, looking for the door. "When I come to pay the rent."

I related the visit, with considerably less detail, to Helen. On the first of the month, she paid the rent.

It took a few weeks, but in time Helen and I began to give some attention to the curious conduct of the two girls down the hall. It was obvious that they kept odd hours. It was also obvious that there was an awesome stream of men plodding up and down the stairs to and from their rooms.

Our suspicions were confirmed one afternoon when one of the girls was entertaining a caller, with an incident that need not be sketched here. We realized we had been living in an impromptu, unincorporated bagnio, and we decided we had better start looking for a new flat. While it had taken me weeks to find this one, Helen, oddly enough, was able to locate a new place in about a week.

But her problems were only starting.

Unlike Montreal, Quebec City is strongly French-Canadian. In Montreal the natives have at least a smattering of the English language, and there are few difficulties for the English-speaking tourist. But in Quebec City the majority does not speak, and just barely understands, the English language. Those who do, perfer not to use it except in cases of absolute necessity.

This is regional stubbornness based on national pride going back to 1759, when Canada passed from French to British control. The viewpoint of Quebec Citians is absurdly simple: this is their town and French is their tongue, and aliens put out by these realities would be happier elsewhere.

Despite the Irish name, I am of French heritage. My mother was French-Canadian, and I was educated at a French-language college. At home we spoke French when my father was out of the room. When he entered the room, we would automatically switch to English—our own sad version—in midsentence. My father, who traveled a lot, returned from a trip one day and exploded, "You're sixteen years old and you still say 'dis' and 'dose' for 'this' and 'those.' It's time you learned the language." With that, he packed me off to an English college and I learned the language there and by reading and translating English newspapers out loud.

One result of this dual culture is that to this day I "think" in French in matters dealing with numerals and figures, such as a simple addition. Normally this is a harmless handicap, except when the children need help on an arithmetic problem. They accept my solutions, after a fashion, but they're understandably vague about the manner in which I reach them. As Paul complains: "Decimals are tough enough, Dad. But in a foreign language——!"

Similarly, if I lose my temper and unpleasant words escape under duress, the thunder is frequently Gallic. Where the children are concerned, in this case the language barrier is a blessing.

There's an old chestnut about the matron frustrated by her husband's dream behavior. "He doesn't talk in his sleep," she complained. "He just lies there and smiles." In extreme weariness I may sometimes mumble in my sleep, and when I do, the words are French. In the early months, Helen kept a French-English dictionary by the bedside table, but by the time she had turned on the light and riffled to the right page, I'd be awake. She gave that up early in the game.

Most of my work as a newsman in Quebec City was conducted in French, and my contacts and acquaintances were French. Unfortunately, Helen didn't speak a word of it.

This made her life in Quebec City something of an ordeal. She had difficulty making a simple purchase in the drugstore without some grotesque one-sided sign language which often led nowhere. In desperation, she took to wandering around the counters until she sighted the item she wanted. Then she would summon the salesgirl, grin excitedly, and point.

Sometimes pointing was out of the question. Once she spent the better part of an afternoon trying to buy an egg-beater and a comb. For a long time, at one place, she jiggled her wrist in that circular pumping motion peculiar to the operation of an eggbeater. Finally her arm became utterly limp and she started to walk away when the salesgirl flashed a smile of recognition, retreated to the back of the store, and returned with a clerk lugging an armful of fishing rods. As for the comb, she never got it. I had taught her the word "*peigne*," and she came home with dozen doughnuts (which is "*beigne*" in French).

I had been managing the bureau for some time before our marriage, and soon after I returned with Helen I was startled at the change among many people I knew. I couldn't understand why they had become distant, and it was some time before I learned the reason from a suave, elderly politician to whom I had mentioned the coolness.

"You are a *bon gaillard*, Paul," he explained, "and we consider you one of us. So we feel that you could have married here, one of our own girls. I must tell you that we think *l'Anglaise* is charming. But she is not one of our girls."

To ease the tenseness I decided to teach Helen the language. I took her to the Plains of Abraham on the St. Lawrence River, where British General Wolfe defeated French General Montcalm in one of the most dramatic military engagements in North American history. I pointed to the battlefield where Wolfe and Montcalm are buried side by side. "This is an historic place," I said, "and we're stationed in an historic city. If you learn the language of these people you'll appreciate their culture more, and maybe you'll understand their feelings."

After buying a grammar we started in on nouns and verbs, and on my rounds I told everyone that *l'Anglaise* was preparing to become "one of our girls."

Almost immediately the coolness and distance made way for warmth and *rapprochement*.

Soon after this, Helen and I were dining in the Château Frontenac when my elderly friend spotted us from across the room. He arose—a tall, imposing figure with a wild, white mane—and strode toward us, bouncing and beaming.

At our table he removed his beret, slipped his walking stick into the crook of his arm, brought his heels together (but his spats muffled the click), bowed low, and—oozing gobs of Old World charm—gently gathered in Helen's hand and kissed it. "*Enchanté!*" he exclaimed, his hair falling over his eyes. "*Nous allons l'adopter!*" Then he learned over and pecked me on the cheek. I forgot to duck.

I had expected Helen to be overwhelmed by the gallantry.

She was more like underwhelmed. "Do they always do that?" she asked after he left.

"Kiss your hand?" I said. "The older men do it."

"I mean," she said, "do they always kiss *you?*"

"It's the first time," I said, a little unnerved, "but I think it means you're in."

As it turned out, we didn't progress much beyond the first French lesson. My office called me to an editor's job in Montreal, and we never opened the grammar book again. But Helen remembers one word very well: "*enceinte.*"

Chapter 5

PERHAPS because our very first Christmas together was spent in Mme. Labossière's Quebec City hovel, I have very strong feelings about the family Christmas.

It's too late for Paul, Georgia, and Shonagh, but I'm determined that the smaller ones will be spared the horrors of the annual department store atrocity miscalled the Christmas Parade. The last time I took the brood to this November botch, the top "attraction" was one of those juvenile, one-name one-notes who sound as if they're singing from inside a rain barrel. The one celebrity the children had come to see, Santa Claus, had been relegated to the swinging bucket of the fire department's snorkel, an extension-ladder thing that swooped him high above the crowds below. No sleigh. No reindeer. It was like waving at the man on the flying trapeze, and all the children got out of that afternoon was a sore neck, trying to follow the arc of that steel gondola, and a tiresome view of endless platoons of freezing, half-dressed baton twirlers. There was also a monotonous procession of the year's new car models, which was hardly in keeping with Christmas.

Next time, I vowed, we'd stay home and watch it on television.

The next year—some days before Thanksgiving, yet—the parade was telecast as we were finishing lunch. This one had no room for a Nativity scene, but a place of honor had been made for a float advertising a current movie about a happy-hearted wanton who marries well—the city fathers figuring

43

that the presence of its star would add a seasonal touch to the observance. There were all manner of other showfolk, along with blatant free plugs for various night-club and movie attractions.

"Here comes Mother Goose!" cried one of the announcers, his teeth clacking like crazy in the cold.

"I'm afraid you're wrong," said the other announcer, who had lost track of his notes. "It looks to me like Rub-a-Dub-Dub."

It turned out to be a tired balloon depicting Popeye, but the little ones didn't seem to mind the confusion.

"What's that behind the baton twirlers?" asked Marcia.

"Motorcycles," I said.

"And behind the motorcycles?"

"More baton twirlers. Finish your lunch."

"Daddy," Nelda wanted to know, "what's a snorkel?"

"It's something to put out fires."

"What happens if there's a big fire and they need the snorkel?"

"We just hope for the best, dear. Don't put the prune pits in your pocket."

"Here comes Santa Claus!" shouted Barbara.

"No, dear. That's just a clown—a fat clown."

At this point the movie star rolled into view and I said softly to Helen, "Imagine, advertising a film about a prosti——"

"Frosty?" cried Lisa. "Frosty the Snowman?"

"No. Just an actress. She's plugging a movie."

"No, she's not," Nelda broke in. "She's throwing something at the people."

"Fortune cookies," Paul explained.

"Is throwing fortune cookies a Christmas custom?" Shonagh asked.

"It is now. Will you let me finish my soup?"

44

"There's the manger," trilled Marcia. "Look at all the shepherds, Daddy."

"No, that's a float for a movie about Alaska, and the people in the truck are wearing parkas."

"That's because Santa Claus lives in Alaska, where the snow is—isn't that right, Daddy?"

"It's just a movie. Finish your lunch."

Lisa spotted Marie Wilson waving from a convertible. "Is that the Fairy Princess?"

"No, she's an actress."

"Oh. Then that must be Prince Charming!"

"No, that's Herb Shriner. He's another celebrity."

"Any more sillybrities?"

"There's Brian Hyland," said Georgia. "He's the one who sings that funny song."

"What funny song?" asked Nelda.

"The bikini song," said Shonagh. " 'She Wore An Itsy-Bitsy Tenny-Weeny Yellow Polka-Dot Bikini.' "

Marcia perked up. "Daddy, what's a bikini?"

"Ask your mother."

"Mommy, what's a bikini."

"FINISH YOUR LUNCH!"

Now came the clowns, somersaulting to the melody of "*Adeste Fideles*" played in marching tempo by an approaching band. And high-stepping behind the band was another cluster of white-booted girls, twirling their batons apace with the hymn.

"Daddy," said Nelda, "when they play 'Come You Faithful' in church, will the baton twirlers have dresses on?"

"I don't think they'll play it that way in church, dear. Pass the butter."

Another convertible rolled into view, and towards its passenger, a teen-agers' favorite, pressed the people touchers, coveys of girls with watery eyes and unkempt hair, hands outstretched to touch him. Ever alert for the tenor of Christmas, the cameras lingered fondly on the mooning, tittering reverence. Then came the snorkel holding a rheumy Santa Claus, whereupon hundreds of spectators turned around to wave at the camera, leaving the disconsolate old fellow up there talking to himself.

"Why don't the people look at Santa Claus?" Lisa complained.

"Yeah," Marcia muttered, "why are they all waving at us?"

"Someday, dear," I said, "I'll tell you why they don't look at him any more. Someday when you're older."

These department-store parades and the price of today's toys are two untidy things about Yuletide that would justify a Scroogian stand toward it, at least over its commerical aspects. It's bad enough that some tin-and-plastic items range up to forty and fifty dollars, but parents are subjected to TV commercials whose animation presents an exaggerated picture of the toy's value. "Buy one," thunders the autumn spieler, "and be the biggest hero in your neighborhood!"

With the average family income in this country pegged at $6520 today, there must be an uncommon amount of frustration on the part of parents between mid-October and Christmas Eve, and some disappointments among children on Christmas morning.

The televised display of these playthings is absurd. I have seen a toy rocket introduced on TV with misleading film clip of an actual launching of a missile. The toy then was shown in scale-built setting, its allure muscled up with tingling martial music and sound effects, and the slick patter of an eloquent pitchman. Few children could escape being conned by such a combination.

I have strong suspicions of the music heard in the sound track of commercials peddling toy electric organs; it sounds like a tape run off at Sunday vespers in Notre-Dame Cathedral. And as for that navel-height jukebox, well—anyone for neighborhood heroism?

Compounding the idiocy is the commerical that directs the child to *tell* his parents that this is what he expects Santa Claus to bring him for Christmas. I remember that, one morning when he was about eight, Paul turned up his nose at the breakfast cereal. Some announcer on a children's show, it seemed, had suggested he tell us to change to another brand.

I must say this "telling" business didn't sit too well with me, and consequently Paul himself didn't sit too well for the next day or two. When I was through giving him my impressions on the matter and he had his pants up again, I told him he'd do well to listen closely, because what he was about to hear he would hear only once: as long as he lived under my roof, the household decisions would be made by two people only—his mother and me.

Not that we need them all, but there are three reasons why we don't indulge the children with thirty-dollar toys (that goes for the ten-dollar shoddies too). In the first place, we can't afford them. In the second place, even if we could afford them, we just don't have room for an accumulation of bulky toys. And, finally, even if we had both money and space to spare, the growing-up years with our lineage have shown us that most of these gewgaws aren't worth the cost. We've been lucky: our children seem to have derived more lasting pleasure from the simple things; and I think that if modern parents who feel they can't avoid buying expensive gadgets for their children would think back on their own childhoods, they'd find that the little things are what they remember.

It might have been the first eraser, with a white side for pencil and a gray side for ink, that was kept in the pocket after class and on weekends lest it be lost. Or the first pair of gloves after years of hand-down mittens. Or a mouth organ. Or the bracelet with the first name on it in ivory (it certainly looked like ivory). Or the first visit to the barbershop that signaled the end to kitchen haircuts.

For my part, I still remember the day my mother took me to the store for the black and white oxfords that were the mark of a man. I remember my brother Bernard coming home with a gramophone, and the weeks of waiting before he'd let me put a record on myself (so vivid is the memory of that thrill, I remember that it was a tinny Gene Austin recording of "Ramona"). I remember my first all-my-own hockey stick, a gift from my other brother, Bill (they were ten cents in those days). And I remember my father returning from his many trips, always with a huge brown bag full of peanuts (five cents' worth), which he would quietly spill on the floor while we fell to our knees, laughing and pushing and filling our pockets until the last one was claimed and we dumped them on the table for equal sharing.

I hope I won't be thought an insufferable square, but I have a tender remembrance of my father bringing home an occasional box of Cracker-Jack and the thrill of opening it up for the "prize" inside (invariably we tore open the wrong end). What's more, I bring Cracker-Jack home for Mark, Barbara, and Lisa about once a month, and they have at it for the prize as we did, and the thrill is still there.

For me too.

Because of my job, I get trinkets and samples from publicity men and sponsors hopeful that their tokens will remind me to watch their programs. Over the years I've received enough toy pistols and cowboy badges to start a foundry, along with dozens of ash trays, party tricks, coasters, music boxes, and plastic figurines of just about every performer except maybe Francis X. Bushman. If I were to take all this home I wouldn't be able to see the programs they represent for the pile of junk in front of the set. But now and again something practical—a game or a stuffed animal—will reach my desk and when I bring it home, I also bring home a special problem.

I will have only one item, and often three or four of the brood will want it, and the question is: who should get it? After vainly trying to remember who got the last thing I brought home, I told the children one night that they would simply have to keep a record among themselves and be on their honor in taking turns. But this arrangement collapsed before it got off the ground: when it was Paul's turn, I came home with a puppet that was a little out of his class; when it was Barbara's turn, I came home with a skipping rope, and she's too small and fat to skip; when it was Shonagh's turn, I came home with a football; when it was Nelda's turn, I came home with a deck of cards, and she has two of those; and so on. Now I just do it the coward's way: I put the item on the table, and if there's any growling as to who's to get it they're banished to a bedroom for a spoils parley, not to emerge until they've solved the problem among themselves.

I don't know if this is a common thing with others, but in our family the toy that takes the honors for enjoyment and long use with all the children is the simple, inexpensive box of crayons. Over the long pull and with no exception amid our eight, crayons have provided the strongest fascination between the ages of two and twelve.

For all their allure, such venerable stand-bys as the doll and the tricycle don't have the staying power of amusement packed in a homely box of crayons. Perhaps the creativeness involved and the concentration that crayoning demands provide an outlet for churned-up energies. Perhaps it's pride of accomplishment. Perhaps it's the endless novelty of the thing. Whatever it is, a monument should be erected somewhere in the world to the man who invented the color crayon—if only for the blessed calm and repose it has brought to countless children. Not to mention their parents.

Since we get a genuine charge out of the children's crayoning, we have a more or less permanent exhibit at our house. It all started somewhere in the very dim past when Paul—he was about five at the time—turned in a sketch to mark Thanksgiving. It was a pastoral scene in brilliant yellows and browns with the sun (or moon) going down (or coming up) over a cornfield (or lake). It was a passable effort despite the quaint appearance of three turkeys in the foreground, each with four legs.

"Well done," I said. "When I get time I'll hang it up." An hour later he had hammered it into the wall with a two-inch nail. I quickly introduced him to the wonders of Scotch tape, and from then on, I think we always had a masterpiece or two on some closet door.

The crayons really get a workout on national and religious holidays. Production at Halloween is always good for sundry versions of egg-shaped pumpkins, and for Columbus Day we always get impressionistic stuff that would be appropriate for Halloween (by the time some of them get through with the beards and costumes, poor old Christopher comes off looking like a two-legged Long John Silver). There's a ferocious run on green crayons from March 1 to St. Patrick's Day, and there isn't a card company in business that can match the sincerity and originality of the heart-strung sentiments Helen and I get on St. Valentine's Day. It happens that my birthday is on the Fourth of July, and I must say, it's a unique thrill for a naturalized American to have himself paired off with the likes of Ben Franklin. Each Easter I try to impress on the children the religious aspect of the observance, so they'll concentrate on the Resurrection and ease up on the bunny bit. But legends die hard, and usually the April exhibit will have a weird one or two—like Christ rising into the clouds with a rabbit under his arm.

But Christmas is when their fancies really reach orbit—Santa Claus peering over the top of the manger; shepherds tending their reindeer (that one with the red nose makes the whole flock look silly); the Wise Men pulling up to the stable in a jingle-belled sleigh; Joseph holding up a candy cane; and so on. The warm touch here is that these creations are first delivered to us as Christmas cards, with appropriate greetings; then they're taped to their places of honor on the closet doors. At that, I find these imaginative offerings more fun, more inspiring than most of the costly standard cards that come from people I don't know or can't identify.

I'm referring to the cards that are so vexing—I suppose most people get them—the ones you can't make out. The classic repeater, of course, is the unsigned card; that one you just forget. What throws me is the non-signer who's meticulous enough to write in a message; did you ever get an anonymous card wishing you the very best this merry season that says, "Don't fail us this time. Everybody's expecting you!" Fail what? Expected where?

Almost every Christmas I can expect one of those snapshot cards showing two or three cute children in front of a fireplace. This one will say, "We want to thank you for being so nice to our Daddy and his program in your column." And there's no name, not even on the envelope. Worse than the unsigned card, because you have to work on it, is the undecipherable signature. Who in the world are Alghtydfs and Htrolppqe MacWfgilpteyl? It could be Alice and Harry, but they're not together any more. Do we know an Algernon and Harriet? Or an Alphidia and Homer?

And did you ever get a card meant for someone else? It'll say something like this: "Got your note. Hold your ground, and don't let him get away with it. I always said he was a beast, anyway." What happened there? Who's a beast? Is this something we should know about? And even if we shouldn't, isn't it absolutely maddening not to have the whole poop?

For five years I've been getting a card from somebody in Corduroy, Alabama (there is, too, such a place). It's bad enough that I don't know anybody there, but each year his message is the same: "Here's hoping we can get together before another one rolls around." The very thought of getting together with a complete stranger from Corduroy, Alabama, gives me cold chills. And surely you've received the card from Denver or Boston sent by some obscure person you've long forgotten that says, "Will be in your neighborhood Christmas week. Any hotels there I can (ha ha) afford?" All you can do with this one is scrawl "not here" on the envelope and drop it in a mailbox when nobody's looking. And another annual that shakes me up a little is the greeting from some outfit like Amalgamated Boxcar, Hoist, and Crane Company that says, "We want you to know at this time how much we enjoyed serving you during the past year, and we entertain the hope that we may continue to serve you throughout the coming year." Good grief, it's been years since I bought a boxcar.

The contribution cards ("a gift of $25 will help spread Christmas cheer") usually start arriving in October, and I'm often tempted to write back, "It certainly would, even spread ten ways, and it's my hope that some Christmas we'll get one." I'd dearly like to know how my name got on so many prospect lists, especially groups like the Friends of the Homeless Kiwis (in Auckland, New Zealand). And I can always count on a dozen cards from press agents addressed variously to Paul Monroney, Pat McCoy, P. Malhoon, and Miss Paula Molecule. A few of these will have a nice word about my bowling column or my travel column or my sports column, and will have been rerouted to the Chicago *Sun-Times* from the Baltimore *Sun* and the Toledo *Times*.

But the greeters who really grieve me are those whose cards arrive around January 4 and 5. They've been holding back on their cards, these people, waiting to see if they'll get one from me, and wondering if I'm holding back on mine and waiting to see if I'll get one from them (which is precisely what I've been doing). But it does seem a little indecent, doesn't it, buying another box of cards on the twelfth day of Christmas?

Because of our space problem it's imperative that at least once a year we dispose of broken and worn-out toys that no longer interest the children. I always thought that New Year's Eve was the ideal time to take inventory and throw out the old. But it never seems to work out that way.

This doll here, for instance, that Nelda had been dragging around for years—it barely had hair left to pass for a crew cut; one arm was missing; and it was stark naked. So I ruled it would have to go.

"Oh, no," Nelda fretted. "Not Mrs. MacReedy!"

"Mrs. MacReedy has had it," I said. "Besides, she doesn't look very nice with no clothes on."

"I know where her dress is! Karen found it in her yard once and she still has it."

"You said that last Christmas. When's Karen going to give back the dress?"

"I always forget. Next time I'll ask her."

So Mrs. MacReedy went back into the toy chest (she's still there, the naked old thing) and out came a fire engine that had no driver, no ladder, no siren, no hood, and only one wheel. I was sure this chassis was ready for oblivion, but Marcia wouldn't hear of it.

"I'm saving it for a present for Nancy's birthday! She always gives me a nice present on my birthday."

"So when's Nancy's birthday?"

"I don't know. September, I think. Or April."

So we reprived this unrecognizable blob of junk, but I had hopes that the little dishwasher with the loose door and the missing faucet could be dumped (since I can't afford the real thing for Helen, I get guilt feelings at the sight of the play model). But Lisa stopped me cold, because the dishwasher wasn't ours: it belonged to Mary Jean, down the street. And the torn purse belonged to Eunice. And the parcheesi set belonged to Sybil. And the deeper I dug into the chest, the more it looked like the lost-and-found tent at Disneyland.

That settled it. "Take every one of these things that don't belong to us," I thundered, "and go from house to house until they're all back where they belong!" They did, and the pile went down to normal.

For about an hour. In due course they were all back from their expeditions, squealing merrily and loaded down with decrepit thingumabaubles that belonged to *us*, including Mrs. MacReedy's Mother Hubbard. So the chest never does get cleared out, though I must say it's a good idea to look into it now and then. The last time I looked, I found my cuff links, half a jar of pimento cheese, and a thriving ant colony in there. One morning I came across a long-forgotten piggy bank tinkling with a dollar and twenty-eight cents in change—the very day I was out of lunch money.

Little ones don't like to give up their possessions. A friend once told me of his concern about his small son's love affair with a discarded bath towel which he refused to relinquish. "It's a dirty, smelly old thing and we can't take it away from him," he said. "He holds it to his face all day, and even in his sleep he won't let go. I'm getting worried about it." I had a brilliant idea: each night when his son was sound asleep, I told him, he should tiptoe into the room with scissors and snip a small strip off the rag. "Just a little bit each night, so he doesn't notice," I cautioned. "One morning he'll wake up and won't realize he's left with nothing."

Weeks later I ran into him at a Little League baseball game and asked how the scheme had worked. "Perfect," he said. "When it was all gone he didn't miss it. Except now he sucks his thumb."

While thumb-sucking, among experts with singularly sharp memories, is supposed to symbolize everything from mother love to father hatred, I see it merely as a short-lived reminder

54

that children love the small, simple things. When she bruised her wrist some years ago, Georgia wondered (hopefully, I thought) if it might be broken. Just so complications like gangrene or bone cancer wouldn't set in, I let her have what she wanted—my scarf as an arm sling. For a full weekend she carried her arm in that sling, up and down the street and around the block, head high and chest out, and it seemed to me that what was supposed to be wince of pain on her face looked remarkably like a smile of triumph. One arm sling, I learned, is worth six Band-Aids.

Even a routine like bedtime can become a picnic (well, almost) if there is the perpetual emotion of love in the home, for where love is non-stop, there has to be laughter. And we've found that the one unfailing way to avoid get-to-bed problems is to see that the children laugh themselves to the bedroom and eventually to sleep.

But here again is a game that calls for inflexible rules: we have set hours for bedtime, and the younger ones are not allowed out of bed once they're settled under covers (this last is a case where we simply established Molloy's Law, with no explanations of any sort, at the earliest possible age). There are three bedtime shifts: at 7:30 P.M. the first group, consisting of Mark and Barbara, toddles off, under the surveillance of Shonagh and Georgia, who get the whole job done (including baths) by 8 P.M., when the second shift— Lisa, Marcia, and Nelda—climb into their pajamas. When I'm home, and if a reminder is needed, it's concise and unmistakable: "Teeth *and* prayers!" Anyone who hasn't taken in a load of water by tuck-in time goes without until morning, except in the case of illness. Paul and the two older girls have a 9 P.M. deadline, which, because of their chores, is waived on nights heavy with homework. We close no doors and we don't bring our voices down to whispers. Nor do we tone down the radio or television if it's on; the children slip into slumber to the sound of normal household noise. This often surprises some of our guests when we have company, but I think they go home with new ideas.

On nights when it's expedient, the 8 p.m. shift signals a bedtime story, which today takes almost as many forms as there are children. I started it long ago, when Paul was about three, but some three thousand nights later I reached a point where I could no longer stand myself prattling about elves and ponies and heroes and villains, and out of utter boredom I started making up my own stories. I broke in the act in self-defense, and to my surprise it was an immediate smash. In later years, though, I've had to miss many curtain calls because of my work, and since the show must go on, the three oldest have taken over the last act.

At first I simply improved on standard stories with new little bits of business in plots that had become crashing bores. In the "Three Little Pigs," for example, I didn't like the idea of the wolf eating the first two, so at the first house I had him huffing and puffing himself into a monumental case of asthma which sent him wheezing to his cave with his tail between his legs.

At the second house he developed a hernia and burst two blood vessels from all that blowing, and at the third house (where the first two pigs had joined their brother), I had him falling down the chimney into a vat full of cream when he thrashed about until it turned to butter. Stuck there, he had to listen to the three pigs give him a lesson in good manners and tell him how lucky he was the vat wasn't full of hot water. After that the wolf became the best friend the three little pigs ever had.

My all-time hit for bedroom applause is the annual Christmas serial, which gets longer and more fantastic each year. It started off a few years ago with the power going off at Santa's workshop at the North Pole, and was themed on the youngsters saving the day by fashioning his toys by hand. By last Christmas the plot was cluttered with the Black

Witch from the White Castle (who kidnaps Santa a week before Christmas); Marmaduke the Snowman (who can't stand the cold); Bumblethink, the absent-minded foreman of the toy factory (who always misplaces Santa's bag), and Belinda Goose (who can fly only during snowstorms). This preposterous saga usually gets under way at mid-December and must come to a sensible climax on Christmas Eve. I barely made it to the wire last time out by turning the Black Witch into a frustrated harpy with a heart of gold who kidnaped Santa only because she has never had a toy and was curious as to what Christmas was. The girls eventually rescued Santa by flying to the Black Castle atop Belinda (I whipped up a sudden storm), and the Black Witch moved in with Mr. and Mrs. Claus to become their cook and keeper of conduct records, with the Black Castle becoming the toy warehouse that Bumblethink has always longed for.

I made two delightful discoveries with these improvisations: on nights when, tired or preoccupied, I strike a blank in the story line, the youngsters will join in gleefully with their own ideas on how the action should resume—all the while giving themselves fatter roles in the narrative. I was also relieved to find that ad-lib storytelling intrigued the three oldest. Now-a-nights there's sometimes an argument between Paul, Georgia, and Shonagh as to who will do the honors. The old order changeth, and now I have more time to work on stories I get paid for.

The smaller ones love simple fantasy, but Paul and the two older girls naturally prefer real adventures. While Helen sometimes accompanies me on business trips, we haven't taken a real vacation in ten years. To make up for it, we occasionally leave the suburb for a weekend in the city, and a few times we have taken Paul, Georgia, and Shonagh with us. They're still talking about their last adventure.

For months they had been exceptionally good about their chores and helping to care for the five little ones. Now it was time for a reward, and we shot the works on a wide-eyed weekend in Chicago.

On the train ride into town from Hinsdale I looked out the window, like them, at the scenery sweeping by. I hadn't done that in a long time. And in the vibrant, disarrayed Loop I suddenly noticed the neat-looking policemen on the corners; but they'd been there all the time, hadn't they? And when the elevator lifted us into the neck of the hotel, higher maybe than even the pigeons fly, the children held their breath and laughed with their eyes.

And that night a big man with blond hair and shoulders wider than Superman's smiled gently at them in the dining room as he sang, and the voice of Nelson Eddy held them like not even their teen-age records could hold them. And when the band finished a number, they clapped as if the men had played for them alone. And maybe they had.

From there we raced to the television studio to watch the medium at work, just in time for the ten-o'clock newscast. And the weatherman, P. J. Hoff, who had broken his leg, had them sign his cast, and the newscaster, Fahey Flynn, stayed behind half an hour to show them all the work it takes to put a picture on the screen.

And exactly at eight o'clock the next morning, as prearranged, the man came to the door with orange juice—and them still in pajamas! But only the juice; there would be a walk before breakfast. Then up and down and around at Marshall Field and Company; then lunch; then an hour at Shedd Aquarium and more color underwater than our five imaginations would believe. Then a rest and a shower (so many towels!) and then dinner while sitting near the rink at one of the beautiful shows in Chicago, the ice spectacle inside the Conrad Hilton Hotel. And there Paul danced with his mother and I danced with Shonagh and Georgia, and the way the bandsmen smiled, the kids knew they were dancing well. And that night two of us slept soundly because suddenly our legs were just a little tired.

And Sunday morning we got up an hour later than usual and we walked over to St. Peter's Church with the twenty-eight-foot marble cross in the front, because God lives in the Loop too. And hundreds and hundreds of others were already there, living with Him for a little while.

And then lunch again, and the Chicago Natural History Museum, and the Art Institute of Chicago, where they had been before—but the wonder and the beauty of the afternoon were as if for the first time. And we went home, gushing like the children we all were, and suddenly Shonagh missed her purse with the dollar in it and the dainty white gloves. The purse and the dollar weren't important, but losing the gloves made her cry. And on Monday I telephoned, and the people at the hotel and at the Art Institute and at the museum and at Yellow Cab—they understood. A little purse with a dollar and some white gloves had become very important, and they would look. And on Thursday the little purse arrived in the mail, with the dollar and the white gloves.

A boy had found it on a bench in the museum, and he had taken it to the lady at the booth. And over the phone and in the mail I had the impression that Shonagh and I and the purse were the most important thing at the museum.

It had been a wonderful weekend, though we had planned little of it. But everything seemed to turn out well. Everything always seems to turn out well—most of the time.

Chapter 6

FROM Mme. Labossière's lair with its cocottes and cockroaches, to our next lodgings, near Montreal, was like stumbling out of a telephone booth into Madison Square Garden. It had awesome vastness, and the first grand tour (which I should have undertaken on roller skates) left me with a case of agoraphobia that hung on for days.

It had nine rooms, for heaven's sake, not counting two ornate, high-ceilinged bathrooms and a hall that lacked only a cloverleaf and possibly a Howard Johnson sign.

I came by this hippodrome through a friend in the Montreal office to whom I turned for help the moment I was called back from Quebec City. He found the place, in a suburb fifteen miles from our head office, in about an hour. It belonged to his aunt, a bubbly, well-to-do widow with dyed black hair and laughing brown eyes who wore old-fashioned elastic garters, one of which was forever slipping down her leg.

She was also a passionate cyclist who despised, though she could afford one, the chauffeured, nose-in-the-air limousines that flounced about the cobblestoned, high-society neighborhood she matronized. My first sight of the dear soul —she was in her sixties—was of her aboard her bicycle.

We were waiting for her in front of her second-story apartment when she pedaled in, a little late, with a towering bag of groceries swaying in the basket on the handlebars. She was trying to make time uphill, her eyes darting about the street like hummingbirds, when suddenly one garter spiraled down to her ankle. As she reached over to clutch it, her hat plopped over her eyes, just as the back wheel crunched into a loose cobble jutting from the street like a big black pimple. The bicycle reared up like a fidgety colt in a storm and threw her, cluttering the landscape with celery sticks, bleeding clusters of grapes, and a billow of escaping flour. She was unhurt, and her laugh cascaded off the concrete as we scampered after the canned goods rolling downhill.

"It's not his fault," she sniffed, retrieving a St. Christopher figurine that had catapulted from its niche on the handlebars. "This is a very old street." I was surprised to find St. Christopher astride a bicycle, though I suppose it was all right. As patron saint of travelers, he has as much right on bikes as he has in automobiles, and he'll probably be along on the first American journey to the moon.

(I shuddered through a more bizarre display of symbols some years later when one of Hollywood's more durable actors was showing me through his Beverly Hills home. He introduced me to his cocker spaniel, a sickly, sun-stricken beast from whose gem-studded collar dangled both the Star of David and a St. Roch medal. "Churchwise," the actor explained, "I'm nothing. But my first wife was Jewish and an awful lot of my friends are Catholic, I'm playing it both ways, and this guy Roch is the patron saint of dogs, or maybe it's dog lovers, and it's funny you're a Catholic and you didn't know that, and this medal cost me sixty bucks and it's solid gold, you know.")

My friend's aunt—she insisted we call her "Tante Thérèse" —explained that she was finally taking off on a long vacation, something she had postponed for years. She wanted to loll around the Rocky Mountains in Alberta, and call room service for a while in a tall hotel in San Francisco, and perhaps there would be time for the delicious temptations of South America. Then her ingratiating candor rose to the surface, and she said, "Why should I be shy about it? I'd like to find another husband."

Now then, would we take over the apartment for a few months, in return for a nothing of a rent?

Would we! At this point we would have taken the rear of a moving van if it had room enough to swing a broom in. The apartment had five bedrooms, each at least as large as Mme. Labossière's miserable flat in Quebec City, and the four-poster in the master unit was big enough to suggest a canopied tennis court. But there was more—all of it large.

There was a living room of massive splendor, and the kind of dining room that's generally found in summer camps, and a large den bulging with squat blobs of legless upholstery, and a large kitchen that brought joyous gurgles of disbelief to Helen's throat, and a large maid's quarters (unoccupied), and a pantry that could best be described as a walkaround. Even the door knocker was large, bulging only under muscle.

It seemed altogether too good to be true. There had to be a catch somewhere.

There were a couple of catches. One was Armand, nineteen years of age and—I thought at the time—nineteen feet tall. The other was his brother, François, eighteen, short, stocky, and with the voice of an opera basso. These were the sons of Tante Thérèse's dearest friend in Ontario, whom she was boarding while they attended the University of Montreal. They came with the place like the built-in breakfast nook.

We gave this some thought—all of five minutes, I recall—and decided that common sense argued against even considering such a package.

After all, we would be in the house of strangers, and how could we take on this immense responsibility? Personality clashes were inevitable. We would have to surrender our privacy and, as outsiders, we'd plainly be intruding on theirs. They were too old to handle. Since I worked from midnight to morning, would our dinner be their breakfast? How many hands would Helen need to care for this odd menage? And now that I thought of it, the apartment was too far from my office anyway.

It didn't take us long to agree that the whole idea was mad, dangerous, and impossible. That done, we gave the whole idea of house hunting one fleeting, odious thought and promptly snapped up Tante Thérèse's offer.

So it was that, barely beyond our honeymoon and still in the process of adjusting to each other, Helen and I found ourselves in charge of a readymade family of two teen-agers. We wanted a baby or two early in the game, but this wasn't quite what we had in mind.

Nonetheless, I felt a quaint stirring of paternal instinct when, the day she departed, Tante Thérèse beamed at the boys and said, "You will not forget that Mr. Molloy is in charge while I am gone. I want you to look on him as your father. Understood?"

The boys smiled indulgently. "Understood," rumbled François in a voice that sounded like Friday night at the bowling alley. Armand bent his colossal frame toward me, and I backed away, panicked by the crazy, harrowing thought that he might pluck me off the floor and tuck me into his pocket. But he was just leaning over to shake hands. "*On va s'arranger*"—"We'll get along"—he grinned. For two days after that I typed with the left hand only.

Armand and François were alike in some ways. Both were blond, with handsome, Gallic features. Both shrank from physical exercise in any form (their bus to college was four blocks from home, but when they had the money they taxied to the bus stop). Each had a gentle personality and was artistically inclined—Armand painted and François wrote—and they had the same ambition: both nursed a powerful desire to go on the stage.

But they were the sleaziest, most careless boys I have ever

encountered. Their personal habits were slovenly, and they seldom bathed in the three months we lived there. Most nights they slept, literally, in their clothes; they would remove their jackets, ties, and shoes (when they were very tired they slept with their shoes on). The rest—underwear, trousers, shirts, and socks—stayed on. Their morning ablution, and I saw this countless times, consisted of a sprinkle of water on the face (no soap) and a hurried wet hand through the hair.

They would change their underthings and shirts about twice a month, and our efforts to teach them the basics of neatness fell on earwax. Helen would place clean shirts on their beds at night; the next morning the clean shirts were on the floor. She would smile sweetly and say, "I'm doing a washing; can I have your soiled clothes?" They would smile just as sweetly and say, "We have nothing at the moment, Mrs. Molloy, but thank you for asking." On Saturday nights I would say, "I'll take my bath in the morning; you fellows can have the hot water tonight." And they'd gently protest, "We insist you have the hot water tonight. We'll take our baths tomorrow."

This ridiculous Alphonse-Gaston routine was a weekend recurrence, and they seldom went through with their end of the deal. And this was an odd characteristic of the pair: they were all but unmanageable, yet not once during our stay did they raise their voices to us or show disrespect. If I asked them to do something, they were absolutely charming in their promise to do it. They never did it, but they were so polite in their pledges that it was impossible to explode at them. It's just as well that I kept my temper in check, because the thought of physical encounter with these two eccentrics is something which unmans me to this day.

At one point it looked like we had broken through their untidy armor: François, about to take a girl to the movies, asked if he might borrow my aftershave lotion. I was ecstatic; surely this meant a bath at last.

It meant nothing of the kind. François simply poured out half a handful of the green liquid and sloshed it happily over one armpit, then repeated the process in the other grotto. The reason I fret over this is that François was wearing a shirt at the time, and over the shirt he wore a sweater. But I felt it was a step in the right direction; at least he had become aware of his own unpleasant odor.

Because their hours, too, were disheveled, Armand and François often fended for themselves in the kitchen. Both had ravenous appetites, and they would devour almost anything they found in the refrigerator. They would trundle in after midnight and set out to turn the kitchen into a dripping shambles of greasy wrappings, dirty dishes, catsup-covered homework, and small mounds of varied leftovers.

When they cracked eggs for frying they would drop the shells on the floor, though leaving them at the sink involved less effort. They seemingly had some phobia against covering up jars and tins after use; they would neglect to turn off the gas jets on the stove; they would often take their hideous concoctions to bed with them, staining the sheets with tomato juice and chokecherry jam—apparently able to find blissful sleep in such a mess—they would leave cigarettes on the counters, and they would never, never close the refrigerator door.

I watched them many times munch an apple to the core, then exactly as a baby would, blithely drop the core to the floor. In many ways they behaved like babies, and we could only guess that they had been spoiled by a doting mother and that now the soft life with easygoing Tante Thérèse was turning them into mollycoddled milksops—inept lumps of social barrenness.

What made their food forays so frightful was that they usually occurred after Helen had tidied up after what was our own breakfast, an eleven-o'clock snack prior to my leaving for the graveyard shift. They also occurred at sunrise, when the boys had stayed out all night—how Helen worried about whom they were with!—and in mid-afternoon, when they had slept all day. Thus Helen found herself practically living in the kitchen. But she was too gentle to voice her distress, and in the early weeks I was too confused to catch on. In fact I foolishly believed her when she said she was grateful because all this was good practice at housekeeping.

But their carelessness with cigarettes and the stove constituted a hazard which talk failed to end. I decided on what I thought would be subtle pressure—a Ten Commandments of kitchen conduct that wistfully, and with some pride of authorship, I pasted to a cupboard door. It had such directives as "Thou Shalt Not Dip the Butter Knife in the Jelly Jar" and "Thou Shalt Keep the Bread Covered at All Times, Preferably in the Bread Box."

The next day there appeared this notation, in red pencil, beneath my commandments: "Translation Please. *Ici on Parle Français.*"

It was difficult to rant against such a sly comeback. And while my maneuver didn't shame them into neatness, at least it nagged them into turning off the stove and putting out their cigarettes. From then on, they thoughtfully stomped them into the linoleum.

But the tensions, which luckily I could escape by fleeing to work, weighed increasingly on Helen's inexperienced shoulders. The boys, who went through their monthly allowance from Tante Thérèse in the first week, were becoming more and more trying with their requests for "loans" (among other things, they were hopeless movie addicts). And then we discovered that our share-the-groceries arrangement with Tante Thérèse had become totally disarranged.

Tante Thérèse had set up a credit system at a nearby supermarket whereby I would pay for half of the food purchases each week, the cumulative remainder to be paid by her on her return. The boys wasted so much during their kitchen capers that the costs had become exorbitant. But even assuming, as I did, that they ate like four people, I couldn't understand the whopping size of some of the bills I had to pay on Saturday mornings.

Until one morning when I confronted the store manager. "Look here," I said, "my wife says we've been overcharged by at least thirty dollars, and she says this isn't the first time. There's something funny going on here!"

"That's what I've been thinking," said the manager.

"What do you mean?" I said.

"You folks seem to throw a lot of parties for the college crowd," he smiled—evilly, I thought. "And beer's pretty expensive."

"But I haven't thrown a party since I moved here," I protested.

"Maybe you don't throw parties," the manager said. "But those boys—they throw parties."

It turned out that Armand and François had been using Tante Thérèse's credit for whatever their little hearts and big appetites desired. Though the boys themselves didn't drink, they had been buying beer by the three-case lots for parties their classmates staged about twice a week. They also provided the wieners and buns and other essentials—including a small fortune in cigarettes—for their collegiate clambakes, where art, literature, and politics got a thorough going-over.

We had been taken for a long, expensive ride.

Yet again anger stuck in my throat after the boys explained themselves. Armand said they had begged off their turns as hosts because they were afraid the parties would disturb Helen, so they made up for it by contributing the eats and things. And François insisted that they were unaware that I paid part of the grocery bill; therefore they were guilty of rooking Tante Thérèse—not me. I like to think that's the reason I went soft on them. I like to think their hulk had nothing to do with it.

To the limits of physical endurance, Armand and François were night people—part of a student pack whose happiest indulgence was the all-night bull session. This meant they had to sleep days, which meant they had to cut classes, which in turn meant that Tante Thérèse was being palmed off as author of a copious collection of please-excuse notes.

News that François, who had the literary bent, was the ghost writer reached us in an awkward way.

One Sunday we awoke from a long afternoon's sleep and, while Helen started coffee, I went out for provisions (we seemed to be forever out of food in this place, especially eggs). A few minutes later Helen heard a knock and, thinking I'd forgotten my key, traipsed to the door in her blue housecoat. There, with a shocked frown clouding his gently solemn face, stood a short man in a black cassock.

"I ask your pardon," the priest said, inquiring for Tante Thérèse.

"She's in South America," said Helen. "Won't you come in, Father?"

"And the boys," said the priest, looking nervously around. "They are here?"

"No, they've gone to the movies," said Helen. "Won't you come in?"

"Uh—movies?" said the priest. "They are not sick?"

"Oh, no," said Helen. "Why don't you come in and wait for them? They'll be home soon for breakfast."

"Breakfast?" said the priest, his eyebrows darting upward. Then he cleared his throat and said, "May I ask, mademoiselle, who you are?"

"I'm a friend of the family," said Helen, with what must have looked to the priest like a brazen smile.

He looked quizzically at her housecoat for a moment. Then

he cleared his throat. "And you—uh, live here, mademoiselle?"

It was at this point, when Helen suddenly realized the horror of the situation—what with her housecoat and the time of day it was and the mademoiselle business and her cigarette and all—that I puffed up to them with my groceries. Then the three of us stood there in the open door, interrupting each other with gushes of hurried explanations. No longer rattled now, the priest explained that he was connected with discipline at the college and he was worried about the boys' absenteeism—it was an old and painful problem. But, having read his note advising Tante Thérèse that he was coming to call, the boys had naturally destroyed it. We had had no warning.

"This is the last straw," Helen said when the priest had gone. "We can't be responsible for their classes."

"I don't think I like being a father any more," I said a little lamely.

The beatnik craze that erupted later often reminded me of Armand and François, but despite their ways, they were not beatniks. The beatnik is a professional infant who refuses to grow up because regressing is more soothing to the ego, hating society because its realism goes against his fondness for fantasy. But our boys (we called them our boys at the end) wanted desperately to grow up, and it was an agonizing process. If there was an inner revolt, dramatized by their untidy habits at home, I think it was perhaps against the tragedy of their mother and Tante Thérèse trying to keep them little boys by denying them the ordinary responsibilities.

The few beatniks I've known—unfortunates who want God to get out of the way because He interferes with their lives—voice their hatred of conformists. Yet they are themselves the slaves of conformity. Vacant-eyed men and women dressed alike and looking at each other's sullen faces hardly constitute the height of individual endeavor. Because they believe that disorder and maladjustment are the signs of genius, these people want to be recognized as geniuses. But genius escapes them, because they lack its first ingredient, talent, and so they scorn society, not because of its frailties, but because their sloth has beat them into taking the purpose out of their lives.

But Armand and Françios had some purpose; they wanted to write and paint. At least they had something of a goal, and in their clumsy ways they were creating. Unlike the beatnik, they didn't go deliberately from order to disorder, from tidiness to untidiness. Disorder and untidiness were what they had crawled around in from babyhood, and apparently no one responsible for their upbringing had helped them stumble out of it. As children they had discovered that the things they dropped on the floor would be picked up by others, so now in later life they were dropping eggshells at the feet of the world.

But Helen and I didn't think of it in that light in those days, because we were young. So the chaotic kitchen and the soiled clothes and the food on the floor and the lies and the loans and the sleeping fully clothed and the grocery bills and the neglected cigarettes became intruders that crowded us into a corner of the home once so huge and now too small, and we knew the time had come to break out.

"Tomorrow," I told Helen, "I'll start looking for another place."

But when tomorrow came, another place had already been found. I was being sent to Winnipeg to manage the Western region.

"We're going home again," Helen said excitedly. "Home —home— I feel like crying."

But she didn't cry—then. The real tears would flow at home.

Chapter 7

THE three-month nightmare at Tante Thé-
rèse's wasn't a total loss. I know now that living with
Armand and François taught me a lifelong lesson about the
values of early discipline.

Some people who come to our house seem surprised that
everything is pretty well intact and in place. I don't know
what they expect to find, but they appear a little amazed that
no windows are broken and that the walls are uncrayoned.
They're startled not to find teeth marks in the furniture or
jam streaks on the drapes. They seem bewildered that the
doorknobs don't come off in their hands and that the house
is still on its foundations.

Then they gape at the children, awed that we don't keep
them chained to the floor.

One lady was absolutely popeyed to see the toddlers in
our camp use the doormat before entering the house.
"Doesn't everybody?" I asked.

"But they're so young," she gasped.

Another seemed astounded that there were no toys or
clothes on the floor and chairs. She shook her head unbe-
lievingly when we said that we'd simply ordered the children
to keep their things in their rooms because nobody likes to
walk on building blocks or sit on a doll.

"But they're so small," she sighed.

This has puzzled me for some time. Full-grown adults will
spend great quantities of time and effort training a puppy
to sit and lie down. Yet it strikes them as unusual that a

three-year-old can be taught to use a doormat and put away his things. It apparently doesn't occur to them that a dog operates on instinct, while a child comes into the world with a great deal more than that.

So they turn to Helen and exclaim, "With eight children, how do you do it? We have one [or two, or three] and our place always looks like a cyclone just went through."

(That's frequently true. I've seen these homes, and that's the first thought that comes to mind—cyclone. Some are so disheveled and untidy, it's a wonder more men don't leave home. For that matter, I'm amazed that more women than men don't leave home.)

Our answer is simply this.

A home with ten people must have discipline—obedience to the rules hinged on respect for one another's needs. Anything less than that, departure from a sensible code of conduct, must lead to chaos. Without a system set down by someone in authority, you can't run a railroad or cross the street or raise a family. Helen and I believe that authority is not only essential; it is a moral obligation for which all parents must answer—if not in this world, then in the next.

But to become effective, discipline must begin early.

Before going any further, I should say that Helen and I, some years back, read a book on child rearing obviously written by an optimist. After turning the last page we threw it away and haven't opened another since.

Be scrupulously careful, it droned, about telling the child that this or that conduct of his was "wrong," lest he develop a guilt complex. I happen to think that wrong behavior is wrong behavior, and to pussyfoot around about it is the sort of pampering nonsense that can lead a child to scorn the authority of parents, of teachers, and—eventually—of policemen.

And if he's dragged into juvenile court for mugging someone in the park, his defense will often be a snarl that the

72

world is against him. Unfortunately, there will always be some bleeding hearts to agree with him.

The book had further dribble about respecting the child's "rights," his "standing" among his friends. We give our children a congenial home (discipline and love are not opposites), good food, decent clothes, comfortable beds, excellent education at parochial school, and laughter and affection. I don't want to hear anything about children's "rights."

When Paul told me that "the other boys" were getting five dollars a week for their allowance, I told him two things.

I told him I couldn't afford five dollars a week. Some parents have an appalling fear or shame of telling their children that they are not as well off as the family down the street. They've been thrown off balance by a hideousness of modern advertising which prods them into becoming discontented with what they have and miserably covetous of what they can't attain.

We have no such fear or shame. We work hard, therefore there is no disgrace in having less of the material things and almost none of the luxuries. And we've reminded the children that some of our substantial friends don't have (and may envy) what we have—them. They happen to be our luxury.

I further told him that even if I could afford five dollars a week, I wouldn't give it to him. I can't abide fathers who insist on giving their children the things they themselves did not have, which strikes me as an immature way of buying affection. I prefer to give him something I did have—a hankering (it was more a necessity) to go out and earn money. So he has his paper route, he baby sits, and during the summer he can average ten dollars a week as a caddy. As a result, his bank account has often been a great deal bigger than mine. In fact it's been an occasional blessing when I've needed a dollar or two for lunch money.

But to go back to discipline.

73

When Paul was crawling, he naturally became attracted to shiny objects within his reach. It became a question of moving these objects where he couldn't get at them, or teaching him to leave them alone. It occurred to me that what with his drooling all over the rug—and dampening it in other ways—that was about as much of his "rights" as I cared to respect. And it seemed idiotic for Helen and me to rearrange the furniture to accommodate the first baby.

It's up to him, we decided, to adjust to us.

The object he most enjoyed slapping out of place was a silver goblet, a wedding gift that adorned the bottom of the bookcase. Whenever he picked it up, I would remove it from his hand, frown, say "No," and return it to the shelf.

Of course this became an involved matter, because he would immediately return to the goblet. So again I would have to set down the paper, rise, walk over to him, remove the goblet from his grasp, say "No," again (this time a little louder), and return it to the shelf.

This routine had to be repeated four or five more times for the next several days. By that time I had taken to saying "No!" quite loudly, accompanying it with a light tap on his hand. With the tap, his lower lip would tremble and his eyes would glisten slightly—but he was too cunning to give it up.

I would then feign disinterest, but peek over my paper to watch his next move. He would crawl toward the goblet, but now, before clutching it, he would furtively turn his head to see if I was watching. He knew at this point that he was doing something he shouldn't be doing. Satisfied that I couldn't see him, he'd make a grab for the goblet. Again the physical inconvenience described above (and it does get tiresome after a couple of weeks), but finally he understood I wasn't about to relent. He quit.

We didn't put away the goblet or anything else in the

74

house, for him or for any of the seven who came after him.

I have two reasons for relating this affair in detail.

First, a child can be trained in certain simple projects at an extremely early age. The mistake many parents make is postponement. "Let's wait until he starts walking," they say, refusing to concede that laziness makes them take that tack. (My system is not for indolent parents who dislike getting up off their ottoman.) When the child is walking, it becomes even more inconvenient to apply steady discipline, since he's able to get into more mischief. "He's still just a baby," they reason. "Let's wait until he's four or five." At four or five the child has become even more unmanageable, and the parents decide to hold off again on laying down the law until he reaches the "age of reason," which is seven.

First thing you know, the child is fifteen and whacking the old man in the teeth.

Not only that, his most receptive years are gone, never to return. Actually—and I do wish some of the "experts" would start admitting this—the child starts to catch on at the hospital when the nurse places him in the crib and he's alone for the first time.

Second, while I don't know how the system would work for others, it has worked wonders with us. By the time he was in the high chair, Paul knew I was the boss, I delegated the authority, and he had to submit to it. He tried spitting out his food a few times; then he quit that too.

For the beautiful thing about all this is not that the child needs discipline, but that he wants discipline and is happy with it. By kindergarten age he has already reached the comfortable assurance that there is an understanding chief in charge who would know how to take care of him if something went wrong. As I watch the children and recall my own childhood I've become convinced that, far from making the child insecure, discipline begets security in his puzzled, sometimes fearful little mind.

75

We only had to use the system for Paul, Georgia, and Shonagh. By the time Nelda was ready for it, Paul was prepared to start in on some of her training for us. When Marcia's turn came, Georgia was not only conditioned, but eager, to move in as a little mother. And so on down the line.

Not long ago I overheard Barbara telling Mark, "No! Mustn't touch dirty Daddy's ash tray." (She meant Daddy's dirty ash tray.) And Mark walked away from it. Barbara is three; Mark is two.

This early sense of responsibility leads naturally into a recognition of greater responsibilities. Nowadays when we arise in the morning, Paul immediately walks Barbara to the bathroom (followed by a rousing round of applause by whoever is in the vicinity that she did it there and not in bed), then dresses her. Georgia changes Mark's diaper, then dresses him for the day. Shonagh does the beds and Nelda checks Marcia and Lisa (and there's no forgetting that little old toothbrush). By the time they've said their morning prayers, Helen has the breakfast ready and waiting.

Me? Showering and shaving amid all this traffic is enough of a chore. I keep busy.

Similarly, the importance of putting their things away was pointed up to the children at an early age. I don't know what the child-guidance experts would say about this, but we've operated on the theroy that a child bright enough to reject turnips when there are cookies on the table is almost bright enough to begin picking up after himself.

The four who attend school know that their books and pencils are not to be left on the kitchen table when they return from classes; their blouses and sweaters are not to be thrown across the bed or flung over a chair; their games and purses and other personal belongings are not to be strewn across the tops of dressers or pitched pellmell into the corner of a clothes closet.

Ours is a small house, and everything simply has to be in its place, as much as possible for youngsters, else we'd wind up some dinnertime with a stray roller skate in the stew (nor is that too remote a possibility: I once found a small doll stuffed between the back of the TV cabinet and the wall, its small arm twisted into an opening which led to the picture tube. Lisa had figured that would be a dandy way to send it off on a vacation to Disneyland for a visit with the Mouseketeers).

But the important thing is that the children have been made to understand that neither Helen nor I has time to pick up after them. And even if we did have the time, we don't intend to do so, as long as they remain in good health. We are the parents of our children—not their servants.

A couple of years ago, when young Paul played Little League baseball, he fell into the habit of hanging his glove on the kitchen doorknob. When he ignored several reminders, I hid it. That night, prior to leaving for the field, he very nearly had a prostration fit.

"One of the little ones could have lost it outside, or left it out in the rain," I explained. "So I put it away for safe-keeping. I'll return it in two days."

"But we're playing the team that's leading the league!" he protested. "And I'm captain and I've got to have my glove!"

"I don't care," I said, "if you're Nellie Fox and this is the final game of the World Series. Borrow a glove from one of the boys on the bench."

That night Paul's team not only lost their important game but, in a retributive coincidence, he committed two errors with the borrowed glove (when a team captain has to borrow a glove, he learns a little humility). His own mitt, however, never again dangled from the kitchen doorknob.

Cruel? I don't think so.

At the end of the game, as happens at all games, the team

manager ordered the boys to pick up their gum wrappers and other paper scraps fluttering about the field and dugout —the idea being that the playing area must be kept neat for the teams to follow. And the boys, Paul included, cleaned up their mess in gay spirits.

One lesson in all this is that, even at a tender age, the child has responsibilities. To absolve him of them because he's "only a child" is to place a stamp of approval on slovenliness and—more serious—leave him with the impression that it's entirely proper to chuck his obligations onto others. The boy who won't put his baseball mitt where it belongs will often grow into the supine slob who insensibly lets his wife crawl under the bed in quest of his dirty socks.

Again, it can't be overstressed that this regimen must begin at an early age. If Shonagh and Georgia keep their hairpins in their room rather than on the edge of the bathroom sink, it's because they learned, at three and four, that when I reached into the magazine rack I wanted to come up with a magazine—not a handful of soggy modeling clay.

And so, as early understanding touched each new child, guidance by example fell gently into the routine of eating, playing, and sleeping.

When it became evident a year ago that congestion could lead to injury or dwarfing, I arranged to add a room to the house, a tumultuous project I'll go into later. It's quite spacious —our philosophy being that if you're going to dig a hole and build a room, build a big one. It has the closet space we've needed for years and sleeps Nelda, Marcia, Lisa, Barbara, and Mark—not to mention an occasional neighbor child or two on overnight "visits." We call it the dormitory.

Because of its convenience, we prefer that the little ones spend their playtime in the dormitory. But they are not commanded to do so. Youngsters like to be within chatting distance of their elders, so there's no such thing at our house as the living room's being off limits. We're not "saving" the living room or the furniture for company or special occasions. The living room is part of the house, and theirs to enjoy. All we ask is that they co-operate, so that we adults, too, can enjoy it. That means an effort to leave it in reasonable living condition, or at least the way they found it.

When Mark and Barbara tire of their coloring books or some old saucepan they cherish, the natural tendency is to walk away from it. We remind them that they brought the stuff from their room, and it should be returned. Often, of course, they prefer to attend to more important business, like admiring their toes or figuring out some way to earn a Band-Aid, Purple Heart of the droopy-drawers set.

At such moments I simply tower over them, stretch out an arm, point, and expel a well-enunciated bellow, "DOR-MI-TO-RY!" This is to them what "scat" is to kittens.

"All right," Barbara will mumble sadly, "dommy-totty." And, with Mark scampering behind, she'll tote that bale and scat.

What frees this routine of wearisome nag is the example set by their brother and sisters. Similarly, the older ones' adoption of orderly habits has to be spurred by parental example. In this area of discipline there isn't a whole lot a mother can count on if her children continually see a cigarette dangling from her lips while she's frying eggs, or if her own bedroom is untidy. Nor should a father expect ready response if his own sense of orderliness conjures up a Saturday morning at the hardware store.

As children—I had three brothers and two sisters—we were not moved to help around the house under promise or reward or threat of punition. We became aware, at home and from the nuns at school, that assuming our share of the load was the thing to do.

I don't recall too much scrapping over who had to do what. We couldn't afford maids; Mother could only do so much; and it just seemed proper that we should keep her from driving herself to exhaustion. And some of it was fun. I remember that one of my regular chores was as alternate on the washing and waxing of floors. After the wax was laid on, we would bundle up our feet into large strips of flannel and use them as buffers. After the first polish had made the surface smooth, we would "skate" through the rest of the job.

I remember that from twelve onward I was pressing my trousers (Mother always did the jackets because I could never iron pleats on the sleeves). That she or Dad should have to shine our shoes on Sunday morning before mass was unthinkable. To leave a ring in the bathtub or wet towels on the floor was a form of contempt. And woe betide the poltroon who slipped up during his particular garbage week. He got the silent, for-shame treatment.

Not from Mother and Dad. From the rest of us.

But many of today's boys won't mow the family lawn for less than three dollars. And even then they often figure they're doing the folks a favor.

This may confound some of the child experts, but our way of life—respect for our parents which we showed with deeds—didn't "deprive" us of our childhood. Relieving them of some of the daily burden didn't "rob" us of the joys and thrill of growing up. We had plenty of friends, and there was always enough time to play; but mostly there was plenty of love and affection in our home because our parents could put a whole sermon into a smile or a frown, and they knew the mileage of deserved praise.

Many a modern father worries himself into frustration because his son is sixteen and he hasn't bought him a car. Not one of us had a bicycle as a child, yet none of us grew to hate our father. I was twenty-six when he died, and at twenty-six I was still greeting him with an embrace—a kiss on the forehead, not a cold clasp of hands. Because he wasn't my "pal," nor was I his equal: he was my father.

Common-sense discipline based on respect for authority won me several benefits. Perhaps one of them may be of value to others.

Helen and I have been married sixteen years. In that time she has not had to hang up my clothes or put away my books and papers or chauffeur the children (when I'm home) or even empty the ash tray on my desk. She has enough to do as it is.

And I still press my pants.

As for our own group, I hope I haven't left the impression our home is a little West Point under command of some martinet. We are not perfectionists, rattling our children's nerves with an unreasonable passion for tidiness. There are times when there is junk all over the place. There are times when the children, because they are children, will forget and even mutiny. There are times when I wonder if the team isn't going into a slump.

But those are the times when I think how much worse, how impossible it would be had there been no concern for early discipline. Those are the times when I think, with some revulsion, of our stay at Tante Thérèse's.

Chapter 8

THE promotion to Western manager in Winnipeg was nice, but it meant another housing crisis, because living quarters were still hard to find. We moved in with Helen's parents, the late Mr. William Kennedy and Mrs. Kennedy, and I quickly discovered that living with in-laws isn't at all the horror it's cracked up to be. While he respected my profession, Mr. Kennedy deplored the low wages it paid, and he was forever calling his business associates to get me into something more lucrative. I too deplored the newsmen's low salaries, but I liked the work and I stayed put. Perhaps I was luckier than most sons-in-law, but, while Helen's mother was a little nervous about my occupation ("Writers are slaves of their emotions"), and about the pothers into which I'd led her daughter, we got along well. In our marital spats she sided with me about half the time, and I thought that was a good batting average.

Nonetheless, Helen and I were anxious to be by ourselves. After Mme. Labossière in Quebec City and Armand and François in Montreal we were weary of living with others. So for weeks we searched for an apartment again, and finally I was down to following building equipment down the streets, looking for excavations and sliding into the grubby pits to plead with the builders on their sites.

If there should ever be another housing shortage, my advice to desperate home seekers would be to watch for steam shovels lumbering by and follow them to their destinations. One steam shovel is worth six real-estate men.

It was a steam shovel that led me to an Englishman named Horace Walsingham. He was a retired tailor whose wife had inherited a few vacant lots around the city, and he did what many retired men with money were doing toward the end of the war: he became a building contractor. Walsingham, a round, well-fed man with a shock of violent red hair, didn't know very much about building; but his wife had money, and she had the lots, and that seemed to be enough. Walsingham also had a horrid habit of starting almost every sentence with, "I'll tell you straight." You'd ask him how he was and he'd scratch his ribs and say, "I'll tell you straight, I can't complain."

For weeks I had tried to snare one of the three-room hutches in a small apartment building he had nearly completed in St. James, a village west of Winnipeg. But he had a list of applicants that reached from one pocket to another and, besides, he would only consider childless, working couples. "I'll tell you straight," he said, "your wife ain't working and she's just got to get pregnant sometime."

In vain I swore that, not only did I despise children, I had discovered myself to be hopelessly sterile and the patter of little feet could never desecrate his honeycomb. But he had his own problems, and one day he told me how God had totally abandoned him.

"I'll tell you straight," he groaned, "I won't be able to open up this place if I don't find me some toilets. This war shortage is ruining me."

It seemed that nowhere in Manitoba, which is twice the size of California, was there a toilet bowl to be bought. There stood Walsingham's monument—twelve glittering apartments ready for occupancy and six going to waste for want of commodes. An insane notion tiptoed into my head.

"If I can get them for you," I said, "will you give me an apartment?"

"I'll tell you straight, Molloy," Walsingham said. "You're desperate!"

"We're both desperate," I snapped, as the notion drifted into sense. "I need an apartment and you need six commodes. Is it a deal?"

Probably to rid himself of a disturbed mind, Walsingham agreed. I got his list of models, raced to my office, cut our newspaper and radio clients off our teletype network, and sent this bulletin clattering to my bureau chiefs in Saskatchewan and Alberta:

"IMPERATIVE WE SECURE IMMEDIATELY SIX TOILET BOWLS (REPEAT SIX TOILET BOWLS). CANVASS YOUR AREA AT ONCE AND SHIP SOONEST WHAT'S AVAILABLE. SPECIFICATIONS AS FOLLOWS."

I know the thoughts my men must have had when that message hit their desks, but their response was magnificent. Within forty-eight hours they had found them. In my hysteria, however, I had neglected to have them sent to Walsingham's apartment site, and a week later I walked into my office to find six commodes, clearly visible between the slats in which they were crated, in a neat row by my desk. I had also forgotten that one of my superiors was due in for a bureau visit. But there was no hiding place, and when he tripped into all that plumbing an hour later he looked ready to cry.

"Won't you have a seat?" I suggested, hating myself.

I ordered a truck for the next day, but perhaps because I savored an urge for drama, I chose to deliver the first commode personally. This was going to be my moment of triumph, and I was so wrapped up in the prospect of our own home that the idea seemed sensible at the time. As I look back on it now, I can only shudder.

It was late winter and another snow had fallen, and since I was loping along with my head barely above the rim, trying to spot a taxi, I failed to notice the curb. My leg pawed foolishly at the air for a moment, the weight of the thing vaulted me into a monumental pratfall, and of course my precious burden slipped out of my hands.

I was lucky. The wooden slats on the casing burst apart, but the bowl itself plopped into a small snowbank, as if ashamedly trying to camouflage itself. I ran up and clutched it to my bosom like the priceless treasure it was, just as a traffic officer lumbered to my side. The cop and I made a sublimely nervous pair. "What," he wondered, "is *that?*"

"It's a toilet bowl, officer," I said, hugging it for dear life.

"And where," he continued, "are you going with it?"

"I'm taking it to a friend of mine," I said, praying for an earthquake. Then I added something so senseless that I can't to this day explain it. "He needs it," I said, "in a hurry. Could you help me find a taxi?"

"Friend," the officer sighed, "you don't know how much I want to get you a taxi."

Well, Walsingham got his charming crockery and a month later we moved into the basement cell, which, under the circumstances, was like leasing a wing in the Taj Mahal. But we had spiders. Because of squatter's rights, these creatures had easy subterranean access to our place. Big ones, small ones, gray ones, black ones, fat ones, slim ones, long-leggers, short-leggers, and one particularly squalid monster whose parents, I suspect, must have fraternized with toads. We had enough spiders in our menage to corner the silk market.

I complained to Walsingham. Not only did I get nowhere, but he turned this repellent togetherness into a compliment. "I'll tell you straight," he said, "a spider is one of the cleanest things in the world, and it won't enter a place that's not neat and well kept. Your wife should be proud of her housekeeping."

After that I couldn't bear to squish the little beasts, what with their innate good taste and all. But I never could confirm Walsingham's absurd legend.

Shortly after that it was no longer possible to conceal the pregnancy, and until the day Helen went to the hospital Walsingham never spoke another word to me. When I returned from her bedside he was waiting in front of the building for a "little talk" about the new tenant.

I told him that the child, Patricia, had lived one hour.

Walsingham scratched again. "I'll tell you straight," he said, "it's maybe just as well, 'cause you sure couldn't have stayed here with a baby."

I don't intend to dwell on the death of Patricia. The tragedy of death—and it sometimes has a form of beauty—is a personal one, and I don't think the feelings it evokes can be properly transmitted to others. But I do wish to use part of the letter my father sent us shortly after it happened. Because I have found myself returning to it in other afflictions, perhaps someone else who has lost a first child may gain something from it.

"Well, it was not to be, children. The Great-All Father willed differently, and you must take it in that light, 'Thy will be done.' So it is the duty of each of you, with bowed heads and humble hearts, to accept and willingly make this first great sacrifice of your married life. I know it is hard, very hard, but you have one recourse: the great power of prayer. I feel sure that both of you are doing that now. And what a consolation it will be to each of you. . . . So pray and ask the Great-All Father for the religious strength to carry your cross of sorrow. I know it is easy to say that you should be brave and accept your sacrifice. These are idle words to the heart bowed down with care. But we do want you to know that in this hour you are not alone. We feel for you and with you. At the moment your cross is very heavy, but remember this. It is an old saying, and true: 'Earth has no cross for which heaven has no crown.'"

After the first shock had passed, I remember the painful, almost unbearable feeling of guilt—a frightening shadow that walked always with me. I remember thinking many times, there is something terribly wrong . . . I'll never have a child.

I'm writing this in the bedroom because the eight kids are where my desk is, listening to records.

We're a little crowded now.

Crowded though we are, there are some people—and I suppose they mean well—who feel we should add a menagerie to our group. I react unpleasantly when some otherwise sweet soul looks over the brood endearingly, then says to Helen, "My dear, what these children need is a dog to keep them company."

I resent the suggestion that the children "need" anything. They happen to have a pair of parents who love them, and they have each other. All eight have health, a good outlook on most things (including punishment), and, as a bonus, they've inherited their mother's good looks. They eat well (and I have the creditors to prove it), sleep soundly, have lively sidelines; boredom seldom drifts across our threshold. When they kneel at night to talk things over with God, I don't hear any complaints.

A few years ago I sat in silent pique as two ladies edged perilously close to an argument over what breed of dog we should have. "They should have a large one, like a St. Bernard," said one of them. "They're good for protection." (The lady who said this had two unprotected children whom I was forever pulling off the street and out of trees and off the back of delivery trucks.)

"No," broke in the other lady. "A big dog would knock over the little ones and hurt them. What the Molloys need is a Pomeranian, so they could cuddle it." (This lady had one child whom she probably hadn't cuddled since birth. She spent most afternoons at various functions, and the child was a lonely urchin who seemed to smile only in our yard, where it got plenty of cuddling.)

I hope this doesn't leave the impression I'm against animals. It's just that I feel God gave them plenty of room to roam around, and other advantages (free rent, no dental bills), and that putting them in a small house occupied by ten people would hardly improve on His plans. In fact we've had two dogs, both of which we got at the pound.

Of course the children loved them. They loved the first one so much that they fashioned a gay bonnet for her head, and the first time she wandered off on the road the bonnet slipped over her eyes and she was promptly run over by a car. They showered the second one with so much love—like tugging from each end for rights to caress it—that the poor creature had a nervous breakdown and loped off for saner parts.

I've had to turn down people who offered us kittens, hamsters, and, once, a baby alligator, though at one time we kept two turtles, which we called the two Sams—Flot and Jet. One weekend we ran out of turtle food and I spent Saturday and Sunday pirouetting around the house, catching flies. This the younger ones thought was mad fun, especially when I'd stretch on a chair to snare one off the ceiling and wind up in a shuddering fall. After a while, however, it struck me that there was an element of cruelty involved here and I told the children, my arm in a sling, that it wasn't nice to treat flies that way.

I thought it was a decent explanation, with just enough morality to dramatize the Golden Rule, but the lesson was to haunt me for some time. The first time I thumped the swatter down on a fly poised on the custard, Shonagh turned her saucer-sized eyes to me and softly echoed my counsel. "We mustn't be cruel to the little flies, because God made them, just as He made the little children."

For a month thereafter, until the memory of the incident had dimmed, we had to live with the flies, limiting our defense to a limp flick of the wrist and the gentle reprimand, "Now shoo."

As a columnist, I receive a lot of odd gifts from celebrities nourished on the need for publicity. A television star once flew me a frozen chicken dinner from Hollywood. It was only a single order—there's a crisis right there—and I didn't mind its arriving unfrozen, but it was Friday. A prominent comedian keeps sending me trays and pens with my name beautifully inscribed but hideously misspelled. I have received enough ash trays to turn them into a quaint twenty-four-piece dinner set, and once a press agent who thought my name was Paula sent me a frilly kerchief and an adorable lipstick.

To publicize its new slogan ("Chirrup, the Happy Sound"), a radio station dumped a birdcage housing a nervous canary on my desk.

At home that night I looked at the sea of faces that constitutes my family and announced, "Guess what? I got a canary at the office."

The night was hot, the house was hot, and the stove over which Helen was bending was hot. "Who," she inquired, "gave you the bird?"

"A radio station," I said. "Wasn't that nice of them?"

Helen poured nine bowls of soup and a bottle of formula. "A canary," she sighed. "That's all we need now."

Paul's eyes lit up. "Let's keep it!" he cried. "I should have a hobby." This from a ninth-grader who's a Boy Scout, an altar boy, delivers a paper route, and plays second base for the Hinsdale Pony League.

"Let me take it to school," Georgia pleaded. "We can use it in science class."

"Are you studying birds already?" I wondered.

"Of course," said Georgia. "Did you know that the dragonfly used to be three feet long when it was prehistoric?" (I didn't get the connection either, but one has to get used to these things.)

"Well, if we can't keep it, let's mail it to Grandma," chimed in Shonagh. "We didn't send her anything for Easter."

Helen collected nine empty soup bowls and one empty formula bottle. "We've already got two turtles," she chided. "We haven't room for a canary."

"We can put the turtles in the canary cage," suggested Nelda, the orderly type.

"The bird bath's too small," said Shonagh, already losing interest.

"Why don't we make him fat and make money like Mr. Kransky?" asked Marcia. (Mr. Kransky, a neighboring farmer, raises chickens and sells the eggs.)

"That wouldn't work out," I said, beginning to lose my grip.

It seemed to be Lisa's turn. "Leave it in your desk at the ossif," she trilled, "and some little Sunday you can take me to see the nest."

I glanced at Helen, who was trying to slice a pie into ten pieces (it's a neat trick, and it can be done, but you've got to start with a large pie). "Maybe we can keep the cage," I mused. "It might make a dandy diaper pail."

Barbara frowned at the tiny piece of pie in front of her, glared around the table to make sure none of the other slices was larger than hers, and suddenly yelled, "Let's eat the canary!" For just a moment, there, that seemed like the night's best idea.

At least it did to Mark, for he quickly adjusted his bib, rolled his eyes in what looked like weanling ecstasy, and emitted the soupçon of a delicate belch.

The collective bargaining at an end, we took a vote. The ballot went eight (children) for, and two (adults) against, keeping the canary. I don't know what that would mean at your house, but at my house it means the parents won.

Chapter 9

      I DIDN'T mind ripping my pants at the hospital the day Paul was born; it's what I exposed that bothered me.

      I was at the office when Helen was taken to the hospital, and in my haste to help—what if they dropped the baby?—I caught the cuff of my pants leg on a painter's scaffold in the lobby. The split extended well above the knee, but there was no stopping now, and I trundled on, the ungainly thing flapping behind me. I was nervous enough as it was, in the fathers' waiting room, but the way the three or four other men kept staring at my torn trouser added to my jitters. "I ripped it downstairs," I said, crossing my legs uncomfortably. But they continued to stare and exchange curious glances, and then, to my horror, I realized that they were staring at Helen's stockings.

      I was wearing them.

      We had been to the beach the previous week, and the sun had burned my legs to a painful crimson. When I showed up at the office, stiff-legged, one of my reporters, a helpful-hint type, told me I could ease the agony if I cut the feet off a pair of Helen's stockings and slipped them on all the way to the thighs. The silk, he explained would protect the seared skin against the scraping of the trousers.

      He was right, but in the hot glare of other males in that room there was no protection against a red face.

      The day Georgia was born also brought something extra to remember: Helen's mother suggested that the days of apartments—we had moved into another after Walsingham found we were pregnant again—were over for us, and we needed a house. She had been looking at a suburb called Wildwood Park, about a half hour's drive from Winnipeg. Wildwood Park was laid out on a promontory that jutted like a piece of pie, point first, into the plump Red River. Straddling the cape were strands of richly colored frame houses surrounded by small groves of birch and ash. The price was eight thousand dollars, and we could move in with a down payment of seven hundred and fifty dollars. When Helen's mother asked me how much I could raise, I told her that at the moment I was good for seven dollars and eighty cents, but by Friday, which was payday, I could probably go as high as twenty dollars. This must have impressed her, because she agreed to pitch in with the rest and told Helen to wander around Wildwood Park and pick the house she liked. It was turning a child loose in a tubful of jelly beans.

The house she chose had two bedrooms and was a shade of nicely creamed coffee, with green shutters that seemed to blink pleadingly at us. It was beautiful, and I remember squatting down to feel the grass in my fingers and being awed by the swirl and splash of the river nearby. I had always thought that living near docile waters would be romantic.

We moved in, and promptly became pregnant again.

Until then we had lived in places equipped with curtains and rugs and stoves and heat and lawns and sidewalks. In the new house we had to supply these things ourselves, and I needed more money. Finding extra work was simple: the job practically came to me.

I had friends in one of the political parties, and with a provincial election coming up, I was able to line up a great deal of speech writing. Then a strange thing happened: a number of businessmen who were running for office and whose speeches I was writing asked me if I would take over their publicity after the election. One was a hotelkeeper, another managed a large clothing store, a third was director of a fund-raising organization, and still another, a manufacturer, said my only task would be to compose his letters. These accounts were mine, if I wanted them, the day after election.

Sweetening the temptation, the political party offered me the job of public-relations director with an office at party headquarters. I did some quick calculations and found myself with the prospect of becoming a free-lance writer at a starting income of twice what I was then earning. "Just think," I told Helen, "I could be my own boss, head of my own firm."

Only a fool would pass up a chance like that, so I wrote to Montreal and resigned. Then I went back to writing speeches, scarcely able to wait for voting day, the party's triumph, and the presidency of my own one-man firm.

The party was knocked sprawling by an opposition seiche that swept to oblivion almost all its candidates, including those who were going to set me up in business. When I called them the next day to commiserate, I got the awful truth: they had dropped so much money in the campaign that the luxury of a public-relations man was out of the question for a long time. But the crushing blow came from the party itself: a new leadership would try to pick up the pieces, but there would be no budget for my services and would I mind very much vacating the office at the end of the week? In my haste to go places I had leaped too far; I was out of a job.

All I could do was swallow my pride and return to the news agency. Now, however, I was no longer captain; I was just one of the crew, and since there was lost ground to make up, I found a second job—writing newscasts at night for a radio station.

But because my self-induced demotion was unpleasant, and the fifteen-hour day was wrecking my morale, I found myself drawn to a little flame that had often warmed me—the lure of the United States. After seven years as a newsman in Canada, my salary still wasn't much more than what I had earned at the bottom of the mines, and it was obvious to me that there was more opportunity with the livelier, more dynamic American press. Besides, I had long been impressed by the live-wire, good-humored go of the Americans I had met; they seemed to throw sparks all the time. And since I'd become disenchanted with the long Canadian winters, there lurked, in the little attic of the mind where impulses hide, an urge to migrate to one of the smaller cities on which I'd developed a crush.

The city was Tulsa, and the crush flowered from what I had read about its beauty and warmth in books and magazines, and from what I had heard from people who had been there. I wouldn't recommend to others this system for such a serious step as changing jobs and countries, but that's the way I did it. I took a two-week subscription to the evening paper, the Tulsa *Tribune*, and studied it. I liked its blend of youthful vigor and maturity; I liked the concise, earnest sparkle of its editorial page, free of the pompous vapidity that strangles so many such sections. So I wrote to the editor, Jenkin Lloyd Jones, told him my background, and asked for a job. My luck, I thought, might change.

It changed a few mornings later. A neighbor backed out of his driveway and over Georgia's body, splitting her thighbone as if it had been a small stick. She spent that winter (1950) in Saint Boniface Hospital, across the Red River from home.

Spring was four weeks old and still the wet snowfalls continued to swell the long, full belly of water swirling across the Red River Valley. Then the snows turned to endless rain and the waters that had spilled across the Dakota flatlands surged across the border to join the runoff from the valley thaws, sloshing over town after town—first Emerson,

94

then Letellier, then Saint Jean Baptiste, then Morris—a dirty-bronze fist slamming into pitiful dikes, ripping the sandbags and scattering their granulated guts into the ooze.

Now the rise of the river was more than an inch an hour, and the prairie people could no longer hold their homes. They left their cattle, crazed with fear and hunger, to the deluge in the lowlands. And they fled, eighty thousand of them, northward to Winnipeg, where three hundred thousand others dragged their heavy waders through the muddy heave, piling sandbags ever higher, measuring the rise and counting the hours. And for some that I saw it was a first time for prayer.

Our own dike was a two-mile wall which stood ten feet high and thirty-five feet wide in some places, and for ten days the men of Wildwood Park had patrolled it around the clock, hoping it would hold (I was in the numb position of having to fight the flood and write it up at the same time). But the constant pounding had weakened all defenses, and at midafternoon one day the word went out that Wildwood Park would fall by twilight, and we lifted our women—including Helen, seven months pregnant—and children into trucks and sent them out of the suburb and into the city. This done, we pulled and pushed and dragged our belongings to the second floor of our homes, and hung our cars from tree branches like big toys swaying from chains, and back upstairs we stood at the windows, unbelieving.

Now the ugly dark waters were at the village door, and there was no strength left in the barricade; the sand and sweat and curse and stone that had been the dike gave way. The torrent gushed over the sandbags, and ran swiftly over the brown winter grass; then it covered the shrubbery, rushed into the basements and filled them, it slapped at doorways, then the window sills, and the rise went on for hours.

When dawn wisped away the darkness we were still at the windows. Below was the flood—fifteen feet of it—and coursing between the homes was a grotesque fleet of garbage cans and garage doors. Then the boats came and took us away.

The fall of Wildwood Park, the first suburb to go, brought a proclamation that the city was in a state of emergency. The government turned Winnipeg over to the Army, and into the chilled homes came the Army's first directive: *"Flood stage for the Red River is 17 feet. The level is now 29 feet. All women and children are urged to evacuate the city. Total evacuation of the city will be effected by the military at 32.5 feet."*

Twelve hours after the death of our suburb every dike surrounding Winnipeg collapsed, and in the next three days a hundred and sixty thousand people fled westward to Saskatchewan and Alberta by bus, train, and plane. We had taken refuge in the home of Helen's mother, safe in the city's west end.

Then came the black day.

The swollen Seine River in adjoining Saint Boniface spilled its banks, joining the Red in a rampage that meant the immediate evacuation of the two hospitals in Saint Boniface, including the one where Georgia lay with her legs in traction. There was no longer any communication between the two cities: the three bridges were out, and so were the telephone lines.

Despite all my newsman's connections and pull with the city police, the provincial (state) police, the Army, and other groups, I was unable to find anyone who could tell me where Georgia was. For a full twenty-four hours we lost compete touch with the child; all I could learn was that she had been evacuated somewhere.

Late the next day I found her, safe in General Hospital in the west end. The eighteen hundred patients in Saint Boniface Hospital had been taken across the river in barges by the Army Medical Corps. Most of them had been airlifted to Saskatchewan; the ones left behind were those who couldn't be flown—iron-lung cases and Georgia, because of her fragile rope-and-pulley posture.

A few days later the heavens wrung themselves out and the rains finally came to an end, holding the rise at 30.3 feet. Though the waters did not recede for another week, the flood was over, after the greatest fight against water in the history of Canada. The toll: twenty-four thousand homes destroyed in the city alone, but only three drownings.

After mail service had resumed, I came upon a letter from Mr. Jones in Tulsa. Could I come down after the flood was over?

"It's your first job in the United States," Helen said. "You can't make them wait."

For seven days the water stayed where it was, like a bully who has floored a weakling and won't get off the whimpering body. Then, having gnawed its fill inside the homes, it finally withdrew to whence it had come. Few women whose homes had been hit were able to cross the threshold again without breaking into tears. Under the corroding, hardwood floors had buckled like matchsticks, as if some monstrous giant had stomped them, and the watermark in our living room stood at six feet, two inches.

For me, the ordeal was over, but it had longer to go for Helen. After government pumps had emptied the basement, I set out on the Great Migration and Helen set about scraping the silt out of the floor and walls, scouring, washing, disinfecting, and airing, cleaning the clothes and linen destined for Tulsa and removing our belongings that were crammed ceiling high, safe but musty, on the second floor.

Then, operating from her mother's home, she occupied herself with such things as calling on the U. S. Consul, collecting affidavits, signing immigration papers, filling out questionnaires on property damage, sitting for passport pictures, pursuing the dismal prospect of selling what was left of the house, and writing me cheerful letters about how well things were.

Then she went into the hospital and gave birth to Shonagh.

At that, we had a stroke of luck. They rolled Georgia's bed into the maternity ward, and she had company when Shonagh was in the nursery.

Chapter 10

EVERYWHERE I looked in Tulsa, there was opportunity.

Because Helen was still in Winnipeg, I had plenty of time to think about how heavy a man's loneliness can be. One night I was especially depressed by a radio newscast in which all the news was bad—tornadoes in the Panhandle, court battles, traffic accidents, fires, and general gloom on the world fronts. I went to sleep fretting that the nice, warm things people do, the nice, warm things that happen all the time, seldom got newscast mention. I awoke with the idea that there should be an audience for a once-a-week newscast devoted solely to those things. After work that day I hustled off to the radio station nearest my office and described the idea to the manager.

"And where will you get news like that?" he asked.

I told him that I had worked five years for a news agency and I knew that dozens of those items came through each week, but radio stations seldom used them. If I needed more, I explained, I could get them from the pages of weekly newspapers in various parts of the state.

I was given a tryout, and after the second broadcast the station sold the program to the local bus company, Tulsa City Lines, and paid me twenty-five dollars a show. Opportunity.

After watching television for some time it occurred to me that the medium was passing up a natural—discussion at the adult level of important themes by competent authorities who'd be willing to appear at no fee. I took the idea to the TV station manager, offering to produce the programs, select the subject matter, and round up the experts. The station gave me a weekly half hour, a director, two cameramen, fifty dollars a week, and the chance to pioneer a format which in the ten years since has become a giant of intellectual programming. Opportunity.

After completing a twelve-part series on welfare abuses throughout Oklahoma for the *Tribune*, I asked Mr. Jones if I could develop the exposé further and offer it to a magazine. He gave his permission, I submitted it to the *Saturday Evening Post* and received a check for nine hundred dollars. Opportunity.

When the regional correspondent for *Time* and *Life* magazines left town for another job, he wrote to New York to recommend me as his successor. Time-Life gave me the assignment. Opportunity.

When Time-Life held a seminar for its writers in Chicago I was asked to attend, and the *Tribune* gave me a week off— with pay—to participate. Opportunity.

Shortly after the seminar I received a telephone call from a *Time* executive: there was an opening on the writers' staff and would I care to spend three days in New York, at the magazine's expense, to look over the prospect? Opportunity.

Within fifteen months of my arrival in Tulsa we could feel the nearness of the day when we would recover from the drubbing we had taken in the Winnipeg flood. We weren't on our feet quite yet. But we were off our knees, stumbling over opportunity.

I've often thought on the great moments that have brought thrills to the ten years I've been in this country—the night Helen skipped off the plane to join me in Tulsa, with Paul and Georgia at her side, and my first sight of Shonagh in her arms; the morning we stood in federal court to take the oath of allegiance as American citizens; the day I went to

Atlantic City to accept the National Headliner Award, or the time I cast my first vote in a U.S. election. But I find myself lingering on what may appear to be the little, less dramatic things. But they were big things of great dramatic moment to me, because they happened in the early months of my arrival, when I felt awfully alone and tortured by a multitude of what-ifs—what if I didn't make the grade at the paper, what if I didn't like my new bosses, what if they didn't like me, what if the customs and climate were unpleasant, what if Helen didn't adjust to this strange, new place, what if I had to go back home . . .

But though I had come to this country not knowing a single soul, I met enough good people in two weeks to know that I would not return home—because I was home.

Not long after I arrived in Tulsa, my mother died. I asked my sister, Dale, who had been caring for her, to bring her to Tulsa—and home—for burial. In the funeral parlor, the night before the burial, I was standing with Dale by Mother's side when two men walked in and knelt near the casket. Then two more came in, and after that they came in twos and threes until there were thirty-seven men—each one a stranger— and they all knelt in that room together and recited the Rosary. As they left I had to ask, and then I learned that they were Knights of Columbus and that one in their group —I never learned who it was—had heard that a stranger in town was burying his mother, and they had come to say a prayer. This I shall always remember.

Frequently on the Saturdays and Sundays that I was alone, Mr. Jones would drive up to my rooming house to take me on tours of the city and nearby towns. He used to say, perhaps because I was a little embarrassed, that he was doing it because he wanted to learn more about Canada by listening to me talk about my homeland. But he was really making the hours shorter, and unknowingly he was erasing the what-ifs from my mind. This I shall always remember.

One Saturday morning, two days before Helen reached Tulsa, the van filled with our Canadian belongings pulled up before my rooming house to take me to the apartment that was to be our first family quarters in America. Parked beside the truck was a car containing three *Tribune* writers who had come together to help me set up the furniture and get settled. They spent that entire day working in the apartment, and by late evening we even had the pictures hung on the walls. Of course, Helen had herself a bit of a ball for two weeks, rearranging practically all our work, but this I shall always remember.

I learned early about American hospitality. Where else could I have received, among the gift certificates from the Welcome Wagon lady, a document that read: "We sincerely trust that you will not have occasion to use this. But should the occasion arise, this certificate will entitle you (or a member of your family) to one free ambulance trip, courtesy of ——— Ambulance Service."

This, too, I shall always remember.

It's quite common for friends to say they feel sorry for me. Not just because I have to watch so much television, but because I must do it with the distraction of eight children. The critic's meditation, they say, should be free from intrusion, especially the runny-nosed, elbowing, this-is-my-seat-go-sit-on-the-floor kind.

Nonsense. Where family (early-evening) programs are concerned, I have a built-in audience reaction, for it's worth repeating that the child is much more perceptive and makes a better critic than most adults care to concede. I've tried to cheat and shorten the bedtime story, on nights when I was tired, by skipping a page or a paragraph. It doesn't work. If they've heard the story only once before, they catch on immediately, and you have to go back and give them the complete text.

I wouldn't pan a program solely on the brood's reaction, but I value the germs of judgment in their interest or detachment. When one child walks out on what is supposed to be comedy, it doesn't necessarily mean the comedy is flat. But when seven file out and the baby gets that hey-wait-for-me-look in his eyes, I get ideas. And I frequently use them.

I don't pick their brains on interludes like "Omnibus." What I'm saying is that with eight children I'm luckier than most critics on programs produced for the bubble-gum brigade. And when my review says that a particular crudity is offensive in the pre-bedtime slot, I have the warm feeling of constructive honesty.

But professionally or not, I like to watch TV in the presence of children principally because if the program is an absolute bore their comments often liven it up. Sometimes it's so unbelievably awful, it won't draw any comment at all, and when that happens, the smaller ones get affectionate and piggybacky, with the result that I've gone through countless shows with sticky hands over my eyes. Looking back on it, perhaps that wasn't such a bad idea.

For a while "Ding Dong School" was a big thing at our house, especially with Lisa, an imaginative sprite with the curiosity of a squirrel. As I was turning it on one morning, I asked what she liked best about Miss Frances.

"Because she cooks a little minute," Lisa said firmly. She thought things over for a moment, and added, "She pretty and she has a pretty apron." She furled Helen's apron about her until she looked like a stray midget at a Bohemian bazaar, and when the picture came on, there was Miss Frances demolishing a couple of eggs.

"We're going to do some scrambled eggs this morning," chirped Miss Frances, struggling with a hunk of butter that stuck to the spoon. She got it off her fingers finally, explaining, "But my fingers were clean, weren't they?"

Lisa, now giving me a running commentary, observed, "She

wiped them on her pretty apron, so it won't be pretty again."

Then Miss Frances got carried away with the greasy project. "Doesn't it smell delicious! I'm so sorry you can't smell things as you see them on television."

This made Lisa giggle, and I gagged, grateful indeed that we can't smell things on television. I asked her what had become of the eggs and she said, "They're melted now on the stove."

After that Miss Frances read a story called "We Love Grandpa" and I asked Lisa where her grandpa was. "He's dead," she said happily, "and he's living by the North Pole."

"What's he doing there?"

"He's living at Santa Claus," she said, frowning at my ignorance.

Next Miss Frances fashioned some cookies out of modeling clay, following this with a display of finger paintings (all fingers) sent in by her young fans. Then she got tangled in her microphone cord, escaped nimbly, and said, "That's what happens sometimes."

Lisa wasn't impressed. "Skip on the rope!" she shouted. At this point there was an intermission and a young musician filled in at the organ. Lisa turned to me and solemnly revealed, "That's her grandpa."

After the show Lisa insisted on cracking some eggs just like Miss Frances had taught her. They wouldn't crack on the edge of the bowl so she pulverized them. "Let's crack some more!" she cried gleefully. I said something about waste and removed the shale from the mess in the bowl, added malted powder, sugar, milk, and a dash of vanilla (none of this had I learned from "Ding Dong School") and we had a milk shake. It wasn't bad. A little shelly, mind you, but all right. At any rate, Lisa's fascination was intense, and Miss Frances was not just a face in the box. "We'll cook again the other day," she said, waving good-by to Arthur

Godfrey, who had now replaced Miss Frances on the screen. "Don't fall on the rope."

Her sense of realism reminded me of the time Shonagh and Georgia were younger. One morning as the program came on, I heard Shonagh scold, "No! No! Miss Frances. Wait a minute!" A moment later her voice rose to a shout. "Miss Frances, not now! Please wait a minute!"

When I walked into the living room Shonagh was furiously slapping the screen with her chubby palm, and her sobs had turned to shrieks. "I told you to wait, Miss Frances! Georgia's still in the baf'room!"

I told the story to a friend who told a friend and some months later it was the theme of cartoonist Cal Alley's syndicated strip, "The Ryatts." A few years later I was interviewing Miss Frances (Dr. Frances Horwich) in her New York apartment when she pointed to the wall in her trophy room and grinned. There hung the original of Alley's strip. "That baf'room thing," she said, "is one of the greatest compliments the program ever had."

Not long after Mark was born I was the subject of one of those Sunday-afternoon interviews in depth on a Chicago TV station. In hopes that I might get a column out of the project, I suggested to Paul, Georgia, and Shonagh that they take on my chores and "review" me. Here are their comments precisely as they jotted them down.

Paul: "I could see the wrinkles on your face. I guess you didn't have any make-up. The other man didn't have wrinkles. (He did too, but make-up hid his.) It went fast because I didn't see any commercials."

Georgia: "I thought you were good. You looked up at the ceiling a lot. You answered all the questions very well but you but [butt] in too much. Were you nervous?"

Shonagh: "It was realy just an orniary thing. You just

sat and talked. But you sounde like an interesting man. And you didn't wiggle."

The reactions of the others were varied. Nelda was disappointed because she had taken it for granted that if I was going to be on television I would at least sing. Her instructions had been specific: I was to sing "Sugar in the Morning" and then, "after the people clap," I was to oblige with an encore on "Good King Wenceslaus." As it turned out, I wasn't able to sing "Good King Wenceslaus" or anything else, and Nelda not only protested all through the telecast; she broke into tears before it was over. So instead of a bedtime story that night I had to sing for a solid twenty minutes until I came to wish, I'm afraid, that Wenceslaus should drop dead.

Marcia had obviously been conditioned to those daytime guestings, because when I came through the door she examined my empty hands, frowned, and exclaimed, "They didn't give you anything!" Lisa limited herself to scooping everyone in sight by thumping the set and shouting "Daddy's in there"—all the while depositing narrow swaths of marmalade across the screen. Barbara was pointedly explicit in her critical reaction: she slept through the whole thing. So did Mark, though he did waken at the midway point, yawned, and broke into a mysterious, toothless grin—the first of his lifetime.

As long as there's no exploitation involved, I don't hesitate to use the contributions of children—not necessarily my own—to bring a fresh approach to my job. It seems to pay off. One chilly autumn the Boy Scouts of Falcon Patrol in Paul's troop had been hinting that I should take them on a five-mile hike as other fathers had done, under "suggestions for fathers." In a crisis like that a man has to think fast.

Anyone past thirty-five knows that the five-mile hike isn't what it used to be. The hills are steeper, the winds are more brisk, and, to be honest about it, the miles are just plain longer. Why not, I suggested, an expedition to a television studio? I told them to select a favorite program and I would take them behind the scenes and possibly get them on the air. They voted to visit an adventure serial show run by one Chuck Bill, a stocky, cannon-voiced ex-Marine. So it was that on a Saturday we trekked from Hinsdale to Chicago aboard a Burlington coach, loaded down with emergency rations of candy, comic books, and sticks to rub together. Why, I wondered, had they chosen Bill's show?

"Because," said Falcon Greg, "it's a long one." (The program, so help me, ran six hours.) "Besides," said Falcon Lenny, "it's the Boy Scoutingest of all." (Bill has long promoted Scout principles on the air.)

I told them that before the cameras Bill would likely ask them to identify their favorite TV shows. Falcon Jerry plugged for "People Are Funny." Falcon Frank leaned toward "Gunsmoke." Falcon Greg mentioned "Science Fiction Theater." Up came Falcon Lenny with a tactful reminder. "Hey, none of those shows is on Bill's station. You want to embarrass him?" (The Boy Scout motto is "Be Prepared.")

At the studio, the boys appeared prepared, except that their shoes were scuffed. Said Bill sternly, "Every Scout should keep his shoes shined at all times!" Then he noticed mine and pointedly added, "Everybody should keep his shoes shined." During the interview Bill asked Falcon Greg about his hobby. "My hobby is make-up," said Falcon Greg (honestly), staring at the pancake powder that had begun to fade on Bill's face. Discovering that Falcon Frank's hobby was stamp collecting, Bill said, "It must be a real job to get a collection like that going." Falcon Frank felled him with this disclosure, "My dad buys them for me a thousand at a time." Hopefully, Bill turned to Falcon Lenny. "Your hair looks nice and neat," he smiled. "I use Wildroot," said Falcon Lenny, and that took care of that. These are the hazards of live television.

After the show we braved the perils of the Loop, bustling with the homeward rush of humanity. Here, I thought, I surely would get the chance to see a Scout help some little old lady across the crowded street. At State and Randolph, they helped *me* across the street.

"We must do this again," I said on the way home. "Where shall we go next time?"

The boys gazed out the train window at the countryside rolling by. "On a hike," said Falcon Paul.

But the Falcons paid me back. A few weeks later a cowboy star came to town on a press jaunt, and his agent asked me if I would do an interview with him. I thought it would be a nice change to have this idol of red-blooded American boys interviewed by red-blooded American boys. Youngsters are curious and candid, and it just seemed simpler that way. I recruited the Falcons to come with me to the suite of the shaggy-haired hero (let's call him McSaddle) and take over —lock, stock, and loaded questions. Firing from the lip, they shot queries at him for an hour and a half and when he took too long thinking out the answers they beat him to the draw and answered each other.

The project got briefly out of hand when Falcon Greg asked McSaddle to name the star who was his own favorite—"when you were younger." The aging performer squirmed and coughed and finally allowed as, "Offhand I can't think of one." Things were going along dandily, with the cowpoke showing the boys how to write with the lead from a bullet ("just like a pencil"), until Falcon Lenny interrupted with, "You're more cowboy than the others. Guy Madison's too thin but you're a little fat, aren't you?"

Falcon Jerry wondered if the ungirdled McSaddle was "the fastest on the draw in all television." The actor started to answer but it was Falcon Frank who spoke up. "They're all fastest on the draw," he said. We didn't stay on that subject, and McSaddle seemed relieved. Falcon Greg wondered about the stunt men. Did McSaddle do all his own tricks? The Hollywood horseman said he did his own riding ("I like the exercise"), but catapulting off cliffs called for a stand-in. Falcon Jerry chirped, "You don't look like you've been hurt much. I saw a real stunt man once, and he sure looked tough." Falcon Frank observed that when it came to falling off horses, he preferred the Indians. "They fall backward—you fellows fall too easy."

How about all that blood when the arrow finds its mark, asked Falcon Greg. "Oh, I know," Falcon Lenny broke in, "they use a sponge."

"Naw," snapped Falcon Jerry, "I think it's catsup."

Falcon Frank swallowed hard and his bow tie bobbed. "A capsule, maybe?" he ventured.

He had scored a bull's-eye. McSaddle explained that a cord guided the arrow into the victim, who was protected by a concealed breastplate to which the capsule of simulated blood was attached. At this point the Falcons drifted into a long, gory discussion of blood spurts and blood flow, and McSaddle, obviously nursing a monumental hangover, excused himself and slunk into the next room. When he emerged, the green tint was gone from his jowls, but the boys leveled a series of questions that had him wishing he'd stayed there. How many times had he been married? (Twice.) Why didn't the gray at his temples show on the screen? (A shrug.) How old was he, really? (Thirty-four—a naked lie.) And was it true that he wore a toupee? (No.)

As the boys filed out, McSaddle led me to the bedroom, where he promptly downed a slug of the kind of gargle heroes don't gulp in front of their young fans. "Good God!" he exclaimed. "Don't ever put me through *that* again. Walter Winchell's easier!" He took another swig, waved good-by and whispered, "And by the way, the hair—it's all mine."

Because of the nature of my work I get a great deal of mail from anxious parents, fearful of the effects on their children of too much of the wrong kind of television. There are great rewards in television, but, sadly, it also has too much mediocrity. Many parents are understandably concerned about what is and isn't proper for the eyes and ears of the little ones. Only two people have the answer to that problem.

You and I.

I say this because the upbringing of children is a seriously intimate business. For years the magazines have been full of the counsel of experts—much of it contradictory—and the more I read it, the more convinced I become that there's no hard, over-all solution to the TV question. You can write up a new set of Ten Commandments (TV-Children Division), but it will be lost on parents whose own video habits lack taste and thought.

When a mother writes to protest that a delicate conversation on a late adult program, or a sexy boudoir scene in a late movie mortified her in front of her nine-year-old daughter, I can only wonder, What in the name of decency is a nine-year-old doing in the living room at that time of night? Why isn't that child in bed where she belongs?

My mail shows that there's an awful lot of we-know-best parents. Commendably, they are aware that restrictions on viewing are imperative, but all they ever do is turn the set off in anger, when a little guidance should also come into play. Snapping off the set isn't sufficient. The parent should make the effort and take the time to help youngsters develop intelligent tastes of their own.

It's foolish for parents to weep over their children's TV tastes when they themselves have never visited an art gallery, or been to a museum, the library, or even attended a PTA meeting. During a lecture before a women's group, once, I was rocked with questions from angry mothers who complained that TV was turning their offspring into vegetables. Then I asked them, "How many of you can stand up and give me the name of your child's teacher?"

The silence was oppressive.

I'm afraid the real danger is not so much that the child gets too much television, which is bad enough, but that it doesn't get enough parental attention. For many parents, television is a wondrous baby sitter (and the baby sitter is a parental substitute) that keeps children out of mischief. They have capitulated to the youngsters' demands because capitulation brings peace. They have turned the dinner hour into a hurried snack during which members of the family eat in silence, their necks craned toward the screen.

There was a time not too long ago when in most homes the first words spoken on sitting down to dinner were some sort of thanksgiving. At many a table today the opening line is, "What time does 'Black Saddle' come on?"

The truth, too late for some, is that the proper molding of the children's tastes doesn't begin when they've become hypnotized by a nightly two-hour dose of groin knifing, jaw busting, and gun slinging. It will have started long before, with good reading, and family visits to interesting places, and at the dinner table and at nighttime prayers, and in the manner and conversation of the elders, and in the smiles and rewards and punishments that are, to the little ones, the sermonettes of the well-run home. In a word, *example*.

Parents who stand the greatest chance of weathering the television storm are those who remain masters of the toy, not its slaves; who educate themselves to the good and the bad of the program schedule; who make viewing a family affair where possible, with consultations that include the children; and who put it down as an absolute law that television will not be allowed to interfere with the routine of family life—including meals, conversation, outdoor play, homework, individual chores, and sleep.

At our house Paul, Georgia, Shonagh, and Nelda have

certain tasks they must perform daily—straightening out their rooms and clothes closets, keeping the yard and carport clean, setting the table, emptying the garbage, making their school lunches, and so on. Marcia and Lisa have their tiny tasks too. Anyone who slips up on these jobs or whose homework isn't yet done simply is not permitted to watch television. I don't care if Walt Disney were to spring out of the picture tube and into our living room, live, with Donald Duck on his shoulder. The children know that under proper conditions there are certain programs they may watch. It's up to them to adjust, for the rule is inflexible.

A child's impressions garnered from the image maker in the living room never cease to astound me. Immediately after sitting through a long-play record (she showed the patience because it was Christmas music, which she adores), Marcia's first reaction was, "It don't got any commercials!"

On one occasion I was most grateful to television. A neighborhood boy hurled a half-brick at Paul, hitting him in the left eye. When I carried him into the house, his face was a welter of blood and the eyelid was split open, exposing almost the entire eyeball. An obstetrician who lived next door rushed in to stem the blood flow, then said, "He's got to get surgery right away." While he called a specialist, I drove Paul to the hospital in near panic. I tried to explain, slowly and calmly, that they would operate on him, and there wouldn't be much time for preparation and he would have to be brave and let them put him to sleep so that he couldn't move while they repaired the damage, and it wouldn't hurt; and as I spoke, my voice trembled and I thought I wouldn't be able to get the message across properly without making my panic contagious—but I went on, telling him gradually what had to be done, and at length he broke in with, "I know what it's all about, Dad. I've seen them do it on television lots of times. As soon as I get there they'll give me a pill to relax me; then I'll put on a gown and they'll roll me into the operating room, and they'll put the cone over my face and tell me to breathe deeply and I'll be asleep in no time at all. Don't worry about me."

I felt as if an aching tooth had been removed, thankful for what a TV remembrance had done to him.

The sad thing about the whole business of television is that its influence and the effects of remembrance can work just as strongly with unwholesome offerings in the home where there is no vigilance over the grayish flicker.

Chapter 11

THE right way to see a new country is by car, even if road maps throw you and clusters of five and more signs put you to panic. For this is the sort of combination that lets you see more country than you'd bargained for. Much more. I discovered this quickly when we motored the 1381 miles from Tulsa to my new job with *Time* magazine in New York. I had it all figured out nicely: through St. Louis to Indianapolis and Cleveland, then a scenic cruise skirting Lake Erie, through Scranton and Newark, and then the Big Town. Five leisurely days.

The plan worked superbly—for the eight hours it took us to reach St. Louis. Then, crazed with success, or lured by some inner reluctance to leave the gentle climate of Oklahoma, I dipped to the right, and we found ourselves in Louisville. This meant that for the rest of the journey I pretty well had to play it by ear, and we rolled into Manhattan by way of Cincinnati, Columbus, Philadelphia, and the Pennsylvania and New Jersey turnpikes—only four frantic days behind schedule.

Well, we didn't exactly roll into Manhattan. At some point in the last lap of the expressway I made the wrong turn, and when we finally climbed out for directions, I learned we were in Ossining. For most migrants, the first sight of New York to put a quiver in the pulse is the Statue of Liberty or the thrust of power in the skyline. For us it was the bulk in the background that was Sing Sing.

I don't know what it is with me about road maps. If I

114

stare at them long enough, the thin red lines and the thin green lines begin to look like a horrid sketch of the circulatory system, and my eyes water. As for those sign-cluttered corners, it's always been my insane bad luck to reach them with seven or eight cars behind me, all of them knowing perfectly well where they're going, and all honkingly upset that I should slow down to take a bearing. You know what happens when you zoom by an intersection that lists Aliquippa, Monongahela, Pughtown, and Pittsburgh—you wind up downhill in the Appalachians.

Besides conceding that I have practically no sense of direction, I should explain that this was our first car, our first trip (jogs to the market don't count), and that we were nearing the halfway point (Paul-Georgia-Shonagh-going-on-Nelda) in our do-it-ourselves population explosion. For that reason I made up my own map after the descent on Louisville, settling on a series of midway marks in a sort of start-and-stop pilgrimage. I decided, for instance, that we were not going from Louisville to Times Square, but from Louisville to Pendleton, which is about halfway between Louisville and Cincinnati. Then, instead of dashing from Pendleton to Cincinnati, I broke it down into a spurt from Pendleton to Rabbit Hash (when friends taunt me about Canadian towns like Moose Jaw and Medicine Hat, which they've never seen, I tell them about Rabbit Hash, Kentucky, and Hot Coffee, Mississippi, which I have). On the Cincinnati-Columbus lap, I put Columbus out of my mind until we had chugged into Xenia. All this, of course, with guidance from the overalled sentinels of the gas pumps that stand like exclamation marks on desolate stretches of nothing. I found them friendly fellows, perhaps because of their loneliness, eager and proud to share the small ribbon of lore that ties them to history.

A foolish way to travel? Perhaps. But I had always thought Daniel Boone to be some fictional hero, like Tarzan, until

115

I discovered in Xenia that this was part of his playground. And I remember trotting back to the car in Lebanon (Ohio) with big news for Helen.

"They've got a hotel here, the Golden Lamb, and you know who stayed there once? Charles Dickens and Martin Van Buren."

I didn't have the heart to tell her that I didn't have any idea who Martin Van Buren was (I could only suspect, at the time, that he might be Dickens' agent.)

There was another reason for liking service-station operators: they were gracious, if a little distant, about letting me rinse Shonagh's diapers. She was fourteen months, so it was necessary to pause often at picturesque brooks and streams. The task wasn't as unpleasant as it may sound, because there's something pioneer, almost romantic, about scrubbing clothes on a rock. I remember kneeling by the clear, babbling waters one crisp morning, happily slapping diapers against a stone and warming all that was lyrical in my soul with the thought that this was the way it was when men lived in caves, and getting caught up in the historics of it all, until I wanted to stand up in that tingling Ohio wilderness and look for Robert Browning's lark on the wing and the snail on the thorn and God in His Heaven; and then I felt the quiet presence of the big shoulders in the black windbreaker, and the tap on my back.

"What," said Big Shoulders, "do you think you're doing?"

"I'm washing diapers," I said.

"You're washing *what?*"

"Diapers."

The silence was awful as Big Shoulders looked me up and down, and if there were any larks on the wing, I couldn't hear them any more. "I want you," he said evenly, "to take that mess and get yourself out of here."

Well, at the moment it seemed to me that I was heading for New York and the Big Time, and I certainly could not

116

let myself be intimidated. "Take it easy," I said. "You talk as if you owned this water."

"I do," said Big Shoulders, moving closer, "and I own all this land. You're on private property."

I collected my diapers and walked quickly back to the car, and from then on, I switched my laundry business to the service stations. We could have stocked up on the disposable kind, I suppose, but they were unavailable in small towns and took too much time to look for in the cities.

Which brings up a poser: what is it about public rest rooms that lures youngsters between the ages of three and six, no matter where we go—restaurants, the movies, church, carnivals? I know most of the trips are not necessary; I've been on hundreds of these expeditions, and most of them turn out to be dry runs. Before we go anywhere I always line them up and direct them to pay their respects to their own bathroom.

So they go, and when we get to where we're going, sure enough, just as we get settled, someone has to go again. No matter that they can't read the lettering on the doors. They can spot a rest room just as other children gravitate to the candy counter.

Once I lifted them to the forty-first floor of the Prudential Building in Chicago to view the magnificence of Lake Michigan and the city below from the observation deck. "Look as it!" I gasped. "As far as you can see—water, water, water. And each time you turn on the faucet at home, you start that water going through miles of pipe into our house, and——"

"Daddy," Nelda broke in. "I've got to go."

"Me too," said Marcia.

"Me too," said Lisa.

"I'm first!" piped Barbara, already tugging at her hips.

So they went. Not only that—four or five adult strangers who had been admiring the lake decided to join them.

117

One afternoon in New York, when the "top four" were the only four, we took a guided tour of the awesome S.S. *United States* as she lay over in Pier 86. The inspection was shipshape until another tourist behind us said in a loud whisper to his wife, "Look, dear, it says here in the folder this boat's got sixty-six public toilets, thirty-five of them in the tourist class."

That did it. I gathered in the four, gave orders to abandon ship, and we hustled overboard as if we'd just learned she was going to keel over.

On the occasions when Helen stayed home with whoever was the baby at the time, I've taken the girls on various outings. This means I've probably been inside more powder rooms than Kleenex. In restaurants and service stations this is a simple matter, if you wait until you're reasonably sure the place is vacant. Then you whisk the little girl inside, sit her solidly, and urge her to be quick about it. The hazard of being discovered, of course, is always there. I can look back on many occasions when ladies (full grown) have walked in on me while I was buttoning up Georgia, and later Shonagh, and later Nelda, and later Marcia, and later Lisa, and later Barbara.

What's to do but smile gamely and say, "We'll be out in a jiffy, madam."

The danger here is that after years of such tactics it becomes easy to forget just exactly where you are. Once, after rerobing Georgia in the ladies' section of a Tulsa service station, I tarried at the mirror to wash my hands and comb my hair (you sometimes get a little disheveled at these tasks). While I was busy admiring my tie, Georgia slipped quietly out the door and outside.

I was giving my hair that final *je ne sais quoi* when a large woman opened the door, froze in her shoes, and jerked her mouth open and shut, as if gasping for air. "We'll be out in a jiffy," I said.

118

One word, finally, thundered from her throat. "Well!"
And she stomped out and slammed the door.

She was waiting for me when I came out. "I saw you in
there," she hissed.

"Madam," I said, "I took a little girl in there, but she got
away from me—uh—I mean—the little girl with me was my
daughter and—oh, never mind what I mean!"

Despite this got-to-go problem—like thumb-sucking, it's
solved by growth—taking the children to public places has
never really been the great nuisance it's generally made out to
be. Two places where I've noticed this are restaurants and
church. We occasionally indulge in the luxury of dining out.
(A couple or more times a year we go through a lean period
when we have to fill up with soup and hamburgers. But
even at such intervals we can still dine out: we go to a drive-
in and have the hamburgers there, and the children are
absolutely mad about these expeditions.)

Occasional visits to a restaurant are good for children, and
they're barely a bother for parents, providing the children
have been taught to keep their place. A family of ten dining
out is enough of a hazard without youngsters playing volley-
ball with buns or disturbing other diners with loud chatter.

There are simple rules. Paul, Georgia, Shonagh, and Nelda
are permitted to select their orders, but under no condition
may they change their minds once the order has gone to
the kitchen. The fact that we may start with a cocktail now
and then doesn't mean that the children can eat every soda
cracker in sight, which they would like to do.

When we first enter a restaurant we've never been to before I sometimes get a turn at the initial reaction.

If it's staffed by waitresses there usually isn't much of a
problem, but when waiters are manning the place, the ardor
of the welcome is sometimes less than smashing. I've pierced
their pained expressions and translated their "How many,
please?" into "Oh God, why me?" Once I saw two of them

skulking behind the swinging kitchen doors, tossing a coin to see who'd be stuck with us.

Soon after the account of my National Headliner Award appeared in the newspapers, I received one of those standard congratulatory cards from a restaurant with this message: "To celebrate your achievement we invite you and your family to be our guests for dinner." It was one of those chic places where the water pourers have assistants (ice-bucket carriers), who in turn have assistants (ice-bucket fillers), and where the tomato juice rates a Polynesian name and $1.05.

Not long after the card arrived I called the manager to tell him when we'd be over, and to request two high chairs. As we drove over on the appointed night (it happened to be Marcia's birthday) I asked for silence, stared into the rearview mirror at the assembly in the back seat, and spoke. "Now, where we're going you'll be getting a meal that probably costs four dollars. I don't want to see it go to waste for gorging on junk. So there'll be no crackers—not *one* cracker tonight—and anyone who so much as mentions the word gets his bottom warmed. And absolutely no orders will be changed. Anybody who asks for a change also gets his bottom warmed. Is that clear?"

When we reached the restaurant I had a feeling that things might get gnarled after we left the car and set out on the long walk from our parking place to the entrance. Halfway there, a ferocious cloudburst suddenly deluged the area, drenching our best clothes. Then, when we entered the foyer (the restaurant was a cavernous place that could have held the "Ben Hur" chariot scene), the children spotted a novel attraction—a parrot of superb green and yellow plumage, the first one I've seen that could formulate phrases. It was capable of three: "Hello there," "So long now," and (good grief) "Cracker coming up."

The children clustered immediately around the cage.

"Cracker coming up!" the hoarse beast shrilled. All that kept me from reaching in to strangle it were those hideous talons circling the bars. Barbara had remembered her lesson well. She eyed the bird nervously for a while and finally shouted, "Get the bottom warmed!"

As we often do in restaurants, to avoid stares, I went in first to install the two babies on their thrones. When the headwaiter led me to the table with my name on it, I found it had a standard setting for four, with two high chairs, two straight-backs, and nothing else. At that moment the manager bounced over. "What a nice little family," he beamed. "Is that not so? But where is Mrs. Molloy?"

"Here she comes now," I said, as Helen appeared in the archway with Lisa and Marcia in tow.

"Oh, you have two more!" the manager exclaimed. "Is that not so?"

"Yes, it's not—I mean—we have . . ." and I let it trail off as Nelda came dancing through.

"Five!" he sang. "Four little girls and one boy, is that not——"

The "not" caught in his throat just as Shonagh and Georgia caught up with the group. Now a puzzled reverence came over his face. "Seven!" The way he gulped, I couldn't tell if it was a question or a comment.

I had to plunge in now and get it over with. Heads were turning at adjoining tables, and besides, Paul—his eyes still on the parrot—was backing in through the drapes. "Not exactly," I stammered. "There's eight of them."

The smile stayed on his face, but he was blanching now, and the menu, which was the size of a tabloid, almost slipped from his hand.

"You . . . have . . . eight——" he said, and I felt as if he'd spotted some silverware in my pocket. "But why didn't you tell me?"

"I did when I phoned," I said. "I told you we'd be over with eight, and we'd need two high chairs."

He tapped his forehead in the classic gesture. "I thought you said you'd be over *at* eight. I made a mistake, is that not so?"

It sure was. Mark and Barbara, weighted down by the rain, had me buckling at the knees, and the rivulets of rain on their faces joined those on mine, giving me a nose twitch I couldn't scratch; and whispers were drifting from the craned necks about us now; and Lisa was polling the group to see if we couldn't just skip the whole thing and go back to the parrot; and I was beginning to wish I had never won the silly award.

The manager regained his composure. "If you'll go back to the foyer," he said, "we will set up your tables in no time."

I leaned toward Helen and spoke through clenched teeth. "There won't be another entrance tonight. When I go through that archway I keep right on going to the car. We're going to a drive-in."

Helen, her ankles splattered with mud, looked at the remains of her new permanent reflected in the window. "Leave a place like this?" she said. "You can call for us when you've had your hamburger."

There was another grand entrance, and I hoped that this time around we would attract less attention. But this wasn't our night.

No sooner had the assistant ice-bucket carrier asked us if they were all ours (sometimes I'm tempted to answer that they're really Brownie Troop 26), than Marcia protested that we seemed to have lost the point of the whole thing—her birthday. "Is today really your birthday?" the waiter said. "Yes," trilled Marcia, who had waited weeks for this.

"Then I have a surprise for you," the waiter said.

It turned out that any diner celebrating a birthday received a small, one-serving cake with one candle on it, brought in at the start of the meal, presumably so it could be admired throughout the evening. Marcia wasn't too keen about winding up with a solitary candle when she had expected six, despite my explanation that six candles would drop too much wax into too little icing ("I like wax!"), and we solved that by letting her blow out the same candle six times. Then came the lusty "Happy Birthday" song, which wouldn't draw too much attention, but for the fact that Lisa prefers to go with *"Frère Jacques,"* which throws the rest of the Molloy Chorale off key (except Mark's monotone chant, which is impervious to anything).

Shortly after I had ordered steaks all around, and immediately after Georgia had led us into the saying of grace, Shonagh looked up a little sadly and said, "Daddy, today's Friday."

"Of course it is," I said. "Tuck in Lisa's napkin."

"But Daddy, we can't have meat . . ."

There was half a minute of silence, and finally I said, "We'll just have to change the order."

Marcia, suddenly fearful that she was going to lose her treat, pulled the little cake toward her and piped, "You said we never change the order."

"You can't. I can," I said. "You keep your cake, but I've got to change the order."

Barbara still remembered my speech in the car. "Get the bottom warmed!" she shouted.

When dinner was over, and Georgia and Shonagh wetted the napkin tips to wipe the little ones' faces, two ladies at a nearby table beckoned to Paul. I told him it was all right to go to them, and he returned with a note for his mother that read: "My friend and I have voted you and your husband as having been the most understanding and wonderful parents, having the finest behaved family we have ever seen. Thank you for letting us see you. Miss —— and Miss ——."

I hesitate about quoting this note, for fear it sounds puffy.

But the fact is we have received several like it, and I mention them because our children do not have superior traits of character. If they are well behaved in public, it's because we've tried to teach them in small easy doses the how and why of good behavior. We have seldom said, "Would you like to do this for us?" To put it that way is almost to invite "no" for an answer. Because, like the parent, the child is an animal—only he is a small, inexperienced animal whose instinct is to seek his own way. Our system has been to make it clear that, as parents, we are in charge of the house and that mutiny of any sort cannot be tolerated. We tell the child we expect a certain basic conduct, and while we explain why we want what we want, at no time do we approach the point of apology. I've seen parents embarrassed about asking their children to run an errand, explaining why they themselves couldn't attend to it. This I can never understand.

"But you must respect the child," some parents will say. Of course we respect the child as a human being created in the image of God, but I have never been able to believe, as some parents seem to believe, that the child's "security" is jeopardized by intelligent demands of behavior and responsibility. On the contrary, I'm convinced that where such demands are absent the child is insecure. He wants to *do* things —this is a natural urge—but the doting parent who wrongly fears "insecurity" has deprived him of the chance to do things for himself, to nourish independence, because that parent is afraid of losing the child's affection. The time for the child to learn that he cannot have everything he wants is in infancy, and the parent who has the courage to tackle this task at that age soon discovers that sensible denial of immature yelps and cravings will not lead to lifelong "frustration."

We discovered by just looking that the child who can pick up food in a spoon and drop it to the floor (or flick it into your eye) is well able to deliver it to the mouth. After the fourth or fifth time, there's no reason for that food to get on the floor except orneriness. And this must be brought to an abrupt stop.

The orneriness of the baby becomes the disobedience of the child and the insubordination and downright revolt of the juvenile, at which point, I'm afraid, the situation is all but hopeless.

We have found our own procedure simple and successful. It must begin early, and it must begin with telling the child what is expected of him. The child will naturally look for the way of least resistance, and disobey. This is where the command comes in—not the harsh, window-rattling scream-command that frightens the child out of understanding, but the command that has calmness, firmness, and unquestioned authority.

There will still be disobedience. There will be attempts to mutiny. This is the child growing up, seeking weak spots in the parental armor, probing to get the better of those who interfere with his comfort and desires. This is where punishment comes in.

For us, two forms of punishment have been effective: spanking in the earlier years, and withdrawal of privileges later.

I know that spanking is frowned upon by a school of child experts as "cruel." But it happens to be my belief that spanking—not to release one's anger, but to correct the child —is an essential, honest part of real parental love.

Except for little slaps on the hand, Mark's turn hasn't come up yet. But with the seven others, spankings have been followed by genuine sorrow—not for having been caught and punished, but for having disappointed us. To achieve these results, however, we have made it a point to punish the child only after he has had the chance to explain himself, and only in the conviction that he knows why the punishment is being administered. And, at nighttime, we have never sent a child to bed, punished and weeping. Sometime before the defendant retires, when repentance has set in, we get together to talk it over, cuddle, and laugh it up.

My theory—and I don't feel it's cruel—is that, if there is to be a spanking, let there be a spanking. A hasty swat in frustration against a corduroyed seat accomplishes little, despite practiced, talented howls. It should be delivered with dignified annoyance six to eight times on the bare behind or on the palms of the hands with an ordinary trouser belt. I remember gratefully that my father never punished any of us in the presence of our brothers and sisters, a respect for privacy which we maintain with our own.

When I was being educated by the Jesuits, we used to get it ("*la punition*") from them too. What I remember most about those floggings (on the hands) was that they were administered by a stocky, somber man who had a severe eyesight problem. When not reading, he wore rimless dark glasses clamped onto his regular spectacles, and he worked in semidarkness, the window blind never raised in his office. He had a peculiar technique: before each punishment he would kneel on one side of the room and the culprit would kneel on the other, and each would say a silent, private prayer.

As I recall, the idea was that both punisher and punishee were seeking divine guidance in this serious undertaking, one to offset the tragedy of an injustice; the other to voice contrition. The students soon discovered that the prayer did nothing for them as a court of appeal: in all my time at the college there was no case on record in which Father J. dismissed the charge and acquitted the accused. But we did use up the prayer time for a more realistic request.

Father J.'s eye trouble was an unfortunate hazard. He had a great deal of difficulty finding the range with his strap, and managed to land on target only about once in every three or four wallops. This meant that we suffered a good many near misses, nicks on the side of the palms and on the finger tips, which, sad to say, didn't count. But they were painful, and sometimes they seemed to sting more than the actual thwack.

So we would pray, "Dear God, don't let him miss again this time. Guide his hand. Please . . ."

There were seldom any miracles, and we often wondered just what was the relation between divine guidance and corporal punishment, because the matter never came up in catechism class. It was years later that I found, in Scripture, that the relation was indeed an affirmative one. For those who insist that spanking is heartless, I pass along these references to it in the Book of Proverbs.

"A rod for the back of him who is devoid of understanding."

"He that spareth the rod, hateth his son; but he that loves him chasteneth him betimes."

"Withhold not correction from the child, for if thou beatest him with a rod he shall not die."

"Chasten the son while there is hope, and let not thy soul spare for his crying."

I know of no clearer summing up on the subject than this observation from Bishop Fulton J. Sheen:

"There is nothing so much that develops character as a pat on the back, provided that it is given often enough, hard enough and low enough. Spanking is one of the most easily understood lessons in the world. It requires no explanation, and no fine points are involved. It is quick, clean-cut, clears the air, allows no long periods of disfavor and helps the parent by preventing an accumulation of emotional worries."

When Paul and Georgia reached what I assumed was puberty, spankings ceased for them. One reason is that it got a little clumsy for me at that point. Another is that the twelve-year-old bottom is a mite tougher than the five-year-old seat. And the third reason is that at about that age spanking is more humiliation than correction. The older child generally reacts properly to the pain of losing a privilege. Cancellation of a swimming date or a movie jaunt works wonders, except in homes where the child is allowed to attend three movies a week. When the child is banished to his room to think it over, it should be for the sole purpose of thinking things over. I understand some substantial parents exile the culprit to his room to suffer amid comic books, the record player, the radio, and sometimes a television set or a telephone.

Where behavior in public was concerned, we seemed to have an easier time of it in church. I was astounded to see how quickly a child will understand the need for silence and reverence in church. We didn't apply any special gimmick, for tricking the child into doing things is to flirt with the danger of crippling his trust. We took no brilliant approach except the very obvious one: the church is one of God's houses on earth, and God being who He is, the most important Person in the universe, we conduct ourselves with even more respect, even better manners, than we show in the home of friends. The child who has been taught to mind his manners at home will almost certainly behave well elsewhere, and almost surely approach the church with decorum and dignity.

Obviously, good behavior is more difficult for the child in church than, say, a restaurant, where silence is not imperative. But it is precisely for that reason, I think, that the nature of the church should be impressed early. It should not be just a change of playground for an hour or so. It should not be, "Mother is going to church and you can come along with her," but, "We are going to church." This is something different, something special, in which the child is to participate as both a duty and a privilege. No dolls. No coloring books.

I've tried to forget—with no luck—the Sunday morning when, in Washington, D.C., on assignment, I attended mass alone. A lady entered my pew with a boy of about five or six and a large paper bag. From the bag she plucked six helmeted soldiers, a tank, two Army trucks, an anti-aircraft gun, a brace of canon, and a landing barge. She set all this hideous green junk on the floor beside me and the boy went at it— "Kuh-kuh-kuh-kuh! SHLEEEEEEEEEeeeeeee-*kapow!* Erk-erk-erk-vaRooooom!" It sounded like Dunkirk all over again as he maneuvered his noisy toys under and over the kneeling bench, pausing occasionally to take aim at my buttocks with his vicious howitzers.

This went on until the sermon, when the little general evidently decided on a strategic retreat. But as soon as the sermon was over, the battle resumed. He wasn't my child, but I was ready to pull off my belt then and there. And I would probably have done so, but it was nearing Communion, which meant meditation and a little something about forgiving those who trespass against us.

I suppose I could have gone through the entire service without losing control, except that I had the misfortune of hooking my trouser cuff onto the bayonet point of one of his soldiers just as I rose to go to the Communion rail. *Hoppity-clank, hoppity-clank,* I went down the aisle, wondering who in blazes was making all the racket and why everybody seemed to be staring at me. It was only when I got to the rail that I noticed the soldier dragging behind me, and stuffed it into my pocket. When I returned to the pew the boy, waiting for me, gave me the most offensive stare and whined, "You took my soldier!"

I handed it to him firmly—bayonet point first, fully expecting him to scream, but (surprisingly) he didn't, and even though I'd just received the Host I no longer felt full of grace. I turned to his mother and, in unashamed disgust, formed the words with my lips: "My God!" Then, in the most ludicrous double take I have ever seen, the poor woman unaccountably got the idea that I was praying, took up the cue immediately, and bowed her head in prayer.

This unfortunate mother assumed that by bringing his playthings to church, she was keeping her son properly occupied. She failed to appreciate how much there was to gain by risking the danger of a complex and taking him off his miserable toys for one measly hour a week—even if he didn't fully understand where he was.

It helps, though, if the child knows who God is.

I wouldn't care to tell anyone when to begin on God with the little ones, and precisely how to go about it. This is a matter depending wholly on the religious leanings of the parents themselves, and on the personality of their children. In our own case, it happens that Helen and I were brought up in homes where religion was not an "atmosphere," but part of the way of life. It also happens that we preferred to start ours young on their knowledge of God. Again there may be a feeling that talking God with a four-year-old is a confusing waste of time. That could be so. But explaining God in simple terms to a child doesn't seem any sillier to me than explaining "choo-choo trains." Perhaps we would have found it hopeless, had we tried to fill the children's minds with doctrine, but we simply told them that God is the invisible Person who put them on earth, their Father in heaven to whom they pray. And that's that for the time being.

I don't know quite how to explain it, there is no standard way of going about it, but things seem to fall into place naturally. For example, Mark (now two) has come to realize that there is a short, serious pause before the meal when we bow our heads and mumble something. For some time now he has been mumbling to himself, and when we close with the sign of the cross he waves his hand gaily around his chest. He may not know, what he's doing, but when he's three, like Barbara, he'll know what Barbara knows now—

that there is some sort of brief attention paid to that strange thing, God, she's heard a little about. Lisa knows we're talking to God. Marcia knows we're saying thanks. Nelda knows we're actually saying thanks for the food on the table and the other blessings. And so on up the line.

The word for all this, I suppose, is naturalness. I don't especially remember the night that Mark toddled up to the rest of the crowd to kneel for bedtime prayers in the "dormitory." One night he was just there, clumsy on the floor and off balance, immensely enjoying what looked like a new game and wondering why everyone was talking at once and paying him no attention. Another night he was kneeling properly, and mumbling. Soon Georgia and Shonagh will have taught him the words.

But none of this—the sight of dozens of little toes curled into the floor as they kneel nightly before the crucifix— would be possible without example. The child should not be sent to church, but taken. I can think of few sights as impressive to the child as to see his mother and father on their knees. It is one of the most vivid and quite possibly the warmest remembrance I have of my own parents.

Getting to church Sunday morning is no longer the hustle-bustle it once was. In earlier days, Paul, Georgia, and Shonagh—who observed breakfast fast so they could receive Communion—would go to 8 A.M. mass. That meant I would drive them to church and return home to dress the others while Helen prepared their breakfast. An hour or so later I would go back to church to pick up the first three, drive them home, and race back with Lisa and Marcia for the next mass. Meanwhile, Paul, Georgia, and Shonagh would clear the table so that Helen could prepare their breakfast. I would return from church and Helen would then take the car and make the 11:15 mass with Nelda. On Sundays, when Paul was

131

scheduled to serve a mass, the Molloy ménage was simply up for grabs.

Now that Mark and Barbara can be cared for by the older ones, it's not imperative that Helen or I be in the house at all times, so we can make a late mass together, accompanied by Nelda, Marcia, Lisa, and Barbara (who now minds my holy orders and sits quietly through the service), thanks to the Panzicas, our neighbors down the street, who ferry the older ones earlier. Soon Mark will be making his churchy debut, and we'll be able to attend in a body—the ideal (and easier) way.

What's more, we'll have the pew all to ourselves.

I hope all this doesn't leave the impression we have a houseful of haloed, dumpling-sweet youngsters. We have had the usual problems with children, though it's not correct that we have eight times the problems of the one-child family. But we have had to keep our eyes on them all the time, and that includes in church, where they can be strange seraphims indeed.

Not serious thing—little things, but an odd assortment.

For reasons that I've never fully understood, the younger ones tend often to break into a strange chorus as we approach the church vestibule. They mean well—we've always encouraged them to sing as loudly and as long as they wish —but it's a little unnerving for others to see them tumble out of the car, lock arms, and swing toward the open doors of the church in carefree step to:

> "We're off to see the wizard,
> The wonderful Wizard of Oz.
> He is a wonderful whiz of a whiz,
> If ever a whiz there was . . ."

And so on. I've tried to get them to switch to some other theme, something that sounds a little less irreverent, but they always come back to it. The only connection I can think of is that there's something castle-like about the church façade.

The special nature of our problems is that they never go away, exactly. We solve them at intervals, but they lie around to be inherited by the next ones in line. We've just disposed of one for the second time, but it will probably make another appearance amid Barbara and Mark.

For some time I had noticed that the ushers at the rear of the church were trying to tell me something but rather hoped they wouldn't have to. Then one Sunday morning I came upon the reason—or, rather, it was presented to me in a basket—the collection basket. As it passed beneath my nose I spotted two white offering envelopes, one with "Marcia Molloy" printed on the front, the other bearing a crude "Lisa Molloy" legend. And next to the dollar sign on both was the figure 10.

By the next Sunday we had convinced Lisa and Marcia to refrain from printing the numeral and their names on the envelopes, thus restoring order to the Sunday bookkeeping in the rectory. Soon thereafter the ushers were smiling again. But I know the problem will recur as soon as Barbara and Mark, in turn, reach that thrilling period in life when they are accorded the privilege of making their first contributions to the Sunday basket.

I use the word "thrilling" because early in parenthood we discovered that when children are given the chance to participate, they're more receptive to learning. The collection routine, for example, which gave them a huge charge, served to teach them that the pastor and his assistants must buy food and clothes and medicine and fuel like other people. We didn't give them this puerile nonsense about the dimes finding their way to heaven, somehow, and to the throne of God.

Similarly, the young ones get a gigantic jolt out of lighting church candles. From this they get the obvious reminder that foreign missions can't operate without money. And though this may sound silly, they also pick up a little something about the handling of fire. Sometimes, of course, they pick up more than expected. Once, after Marcia had spent a laborious time lighting a candle before a statue of St. Joseph, Barbara, who was in my arms, leaned down, blew it out with a triumphant puff, and broke into an off-key andante of "Happy Birthday." People stared, but Barbara, as she always does, stared right back.

On the Sunday afternoon that Mark was baptized, his brother and six sisters were on hand, each with a responsibility (the bottle, the camera, the extra diaper, the blankets, and so on). When it was over, the priest invited Helen and me to move from the baptismal font to the altar rail, there to receive a special blessing for parents.

After the prayer, the priest dipped the aspergillum into the holy-water vessel and raised it for the blessing, and I must say it's a mean-looking object.

It was too much for Nelda. Convinced that some form of mayhem was about to take place, she left her pew and charged rapidly to the rail, where she stomped her foot and shouted: "Now you stop that! Don't you *dare* hit my mommy! DON'T YOU DARE!" Then she caught my eye and realized that the priest wasn't about to conk us and said, less irritated now, "Well, you're getting her all *wet*, and you got the baby wet too!"

On the way home we explained the meaning of this special blessing to the smaller ones. They were impressed. And for weeks after, one particular doll in their collection, a stuffed thing they called Maureen, was baptized and immersed and pommeled (their aspergillum was a soup ladle) beyond recognition. Eventually poor Maureen lost her shape, personality, and about a third of her innards, and we had to dispose of her—a martyr to the faith.

Chapter 12

IT'S not true that New Yorkers are inconsiderate drivers; they gave us a splendid right of way when we finally made it to their town.

Near the city limits a slowly moving truck rolled out of a side road and bumped us in the rear. We were coming to a stop, and the impact spun us just lightly, but it did wrench the back fender so that it dangled beyond our right flank like some wayward silver antler. With cars veering to give us a wide berth we chugged into the honking, swirling heart of Manhattan—gawky and a little scared.

We pulled up near the entrance to the swank, high-toned hotel where *Time* magazine was putting us up until we found a house. Peering over Central Park, it was the residence of a good many delegates to the United Nations, and I can see now why the doorman just stood there, probably making fists in his pockets at us. It had been a long trip, and we were something less than resplendent; it was a sultry, sticky day and the car was cluttered with the things a family car gets cluttered with after nine days on the road—pillows, dry popcorn, diapers, boxes, comic books, nipples, old menus, diapers, soiled clothing, broken sunglasses, diapers, film, and sleepy, cranky children.

And there was that vicious clump of steel sticking out, making it impossible to park near the curb and snarling traffic behind us. And as passers-by stared at us and gazed at the Oklahoma license plates it suddenly struck me that we probably looked like Okies in reverse, and somehow I couldn't very well blame the doorman for suggesting that deliveries were made at the rear.

"But I'm a guest here," I said, triumphantly plucking a piece of luggage from the mess of cartons and boxes in the trunk.

"A guest?" he repeated, his nose tilting up another inch.

By now I was tired and edgy. "Yes," I snapped. "I'm the U.N. delegate from Oklahoma, and I expect we'll be seeing a lot of each other. Now, will you take in that sack of diapers for me—careful, they're a little wet—and please don't drop the formula."

And, the doorman leading the parade with the diapers gingerly at arm's length, we marched into the splendor and the marble of the lobby, and we were home again for a while.

Home was the white elegance of two massive adjoining suites with two of everything, including two television sets and one luxury we would never see again—two bathtubs. And these were bathtubs, not the overgrown basins of modern homes. It also had two sets of twin beds (plus a cot for Shonagh), two huge clothes closets, two telephones and two let's-pretend fireplaces. And soon it would have two nurses.

The nurses came the morning after Paul saw the ghost.

We were a long time unpacking after dinner the first night, and in the confusion I failed to notice that Paul, then five, had slipped out to explore the thick-carpeted tranquillity of the corridor. Suddenly he came bolting into the suite as if pursued by devils, hysterical with fright.

"A ghost!" he screamed. "There's a ghost out there!"

"Out where?" I said.

"In the hall!" he yelled, tumbling over the empty cartons. "A white ghost! And it's coming after me!"

"Don't be silly," I said. "I've told you there's no such thing as a ghost. Now stop yelling."

136

He was whimpering now. "Please, Daddy, hide me. You hide! Everybody hide!"

The door was still open, and I looked into the hall just as the apparition went by. And darned if I didn't step back and feel a cold twinge touch my nape and skitter down my spine. It was a tall, steely-eyed woman wearing a white sari, gliding silently in slipper-like babouches to her room— the wife, I learned later, of a member of a Middle East delegation to the U.N.

It took me some time to calm Paul down—I had to settle my own nerves first—and to explain that the hotel was home for a large number of people representing foreign countries at the U.N. But he wouldn't stop trembling.

At three o'clock in the morning he was still trembling, and I was getting mightily annoyed that the ghost story hadn't worn off. "Get into bed with Georgia," I said. "It'll make you feel better and pretty soon you'll be asleep."

I pulled down Georgia's covers. She was lying there awake and trembling like gelatin on a railway diner. I hurried to Helen's bed. "There's something wrong," I said. "Those two kids are shaking like crazy."

Yes, she was trembling too.

And, in the cot, Shonagh was keeping time with them all.

The moment he arrived in the morning, the hotel doctor came up to the sick bay and soon diagnosed the all-night chills, the high temperatures, and the prostration. "It's European flu," he said. "There's been an epidemic of it in England, and we're getting some of it here."

Paul looked up and frowned. "There's lot of people from Eurip live here with us, Dad says."

I was mortified when I called the office to report that on my first day of work I was stuck in the hotel with the family bedded by flu. I needn't have been. By noon the magazine had dispatched one of its own doctors, who took over with sulfanilamides, hypodermic needles, and penicillin, and all but turned the place into a cozy infirmary. And for the next five days we had two alternating nurses at our disposal.

When I think of what America means to me I start off, as I suppose all aliens do, with the traditionally great things— Plymouth Rock, the Founding Fathers, the priceless freedoms—but invariably I find myself returning to the small things, small in the sense that they were personal and intimate. The strangers who came to the funeral home in Tulsa because they didn't want a newcomer to be alone . . . Mr. Jones, who went from stranger to a sort of favorite uncle in two weeks . . . the reporters who spent their day off unloading the moving van . . . and the concern of *Time*'s top-level executives about the comfort of a neophyte's family— in a city that's supposed to be all steel and no heart, and too big and busy to care.

I was told to stay in the hotel as long as it would take me to find a suitable home. But I was afraid that this might take a few weeks, and I wondered if I shouldn't find a place to rent while I was looking.

"Never mind how long it takes, stay where you are," they said.

So we stayed, and in a way it was an education for Paul. After a year of old movies on television, he had come to learn that men with brown skin and slanted eyes were villains: any goateed Asiatic who wore a dhoti must have a dagger in his belt; any Semite with a turban must have a stiletto up his sleeve. But mingling in the hotel with Burmese and Indians and Chinese and Egyptians, he found that they browsed in the drugstore as other people did; and in the restaurant they ate grapefruit and drank milk; and their ladies paused to pat him and his sisters as other people did. I picked up a bit of an education myself. I learned (though I might have guessed it) that my admiration for Helen's figure was shared by others.

In the elevator one morning I could feel the two Frenchmen behind us giving her the Gallic once-over, until one held his Homburg up to his face and said in a low but audible voice to the other, *"Ces jambes! Ça distrait."*

"Ça se voit," his companion whispered back. *"Et cette taille—c'est quelque chose."*

With that the elevator door opened on the lobby level, and just before stepping out I turned around, gave the pair a roguish leer, and said, *"C'est absolument quelque chose!"*

After about ten weeks we left the hotel. Despite the assurances from the office, I no longer had the nerve to turn in those monumental weekly statements (around three hundred and fifty dollars—they insisted on paying for our meals as well), and I rented a winsome house in Chatham, New Jersey, ninety minutes from my Rockefeller Center office by subway, Hudson River Tube, and Lackawanna Railroad.

The wheel may have been man's first great invention, but three hours a day on wheels is absurd unless you're a roller skate. My commuting time was three hours a day.

But working in New York and living in New Jersey supplied new entries for my what-America-means-to-me list. One was the benevolence shown me by my superiors at the magazine. When I was called to New York for the interview, for example, I had expected to confer only with the chief of correspondents and the personnel director. In addition, I was ushered into the office of the managing editor, Otto Fuerbringer, and then into the office of the executive editor, Roy Alexander. It came as a surprise that the men on the top rung should concern themselves with dining and briefing an unknown quantity that could conceivably fade during the adjustment from newspaper to magazine.

Two years later, much as I had enjoyed the relationship with the editors, I felt that I wasn't doing enough writing. *Time*'s policy was that a writer was responsible each week for only three or four stories in his section, with a trained researcher at his beck and call, leaving him plenty of time (too much, I felt) to relax, meditate, and polish his output. The standing rule was that the good writer was the writer free from professional and domestic pressures. There is no question that the policy is an excellent one for the magazine's purposes, but it happens that I thrive on inborn tenseness, and too much relaxing tends to knock me off balance. More important, I was afraid that in time the sinecure could make me rusty, and I said so to Alexander.

"It's a natural fear," he laughed, "and it'll pass. Why don't you take off for a couple of weeks and just relax?"

"But I've just come back from my vacation. I've been relaxing for a month."

"Well, take another one, and see if your viewpoint hasn't changed by the time you're back."

I cleared my desk and went home to think it over again, and in two weeks I was back, with the same frame of mind. I was embarrassed at leaving at this particular time because I still had a large balance owing on a company loan. Fuerbringer, whose face always reminded me of a big friendly cat grinning in the sun, told me to forget it, and when we parted he said, "If the new job doesn't work out, phone me."

Another incident in New York helped me to realize what a land of opportunity this is. The manager of the Tulsa TV station on which I had produced my series wrote to Lee Cooley, then Perry Como's producer, suggesting that the format should be on a network. Cooley conferred with me and within three weeks managed to sell a cigarette company on the idea. Two years after coming to this country, and with little TV experience, I had an opportunity to have my own program on a national network. But I didn't want to give up writing, and we abandoned the project. Now a novelist (*The Run For Home*), Cooley later was my sponsor—along with *Time* writer Alan Hall—when I applied for American citizenship.

The other example in my what-America-means-to-me collection gained from that interlude was my appreciation of suburbia, that growing chain of landscaped islands held by the young middle class. Someday there will emerge a novel, or a movie, or a television series, or a play about suburbanites that will be free from suburbias. It would be refreshing to read about them as they are—quite normal, quite moral, and quite American.

For a while, in New Jersey, I was beginning to feel like some sort of freak, because I was having a devil of a time identifying with suburbia's oddballs, as depicted by city-bred sociologists and in the novels of some penthoused sophisticates. I wanted to be one of the mob of conformists I'd heard so much about, but I felt like an outcast. I didn't have a barbecue pit; I preferred slacks to bermuda shorts; I disliked patio boozing because mosquitoes and moths took the fun out of it; I didn't stare into my neighbors' picture windows (confound it, the drapes were usually drawn); I didn't borrow lawnmowers or play poker; I didn't earn thirty-five thousand dollars a year, or twenty-five thousand, or even fifteen thousand; I never joined more than one civic group at a time; I had no ulcers—and I wondered if I was antisocial because I had never indulged in wife-swapping. According to the chroniclers who drive by on Saturdays for research on life beyond the city skyline, there was something wrong with me.

Then I started talking to my neighbors about this feeling of not belonging, and I got to thinking of the hundreds of suburbanites I've lived with, and discovered that most of them shared my feelings about barbecue pits and bermuda shorts and boozing and picture windows and lawnmowers and salaries and joining and ulcers. Nor was I ever able to encounter any wife-swapping, and as a newsman I'm nervier than most about asking questions and poking around.

In many writings scorning suburbia, city-dwelling critics scrupulously avoid certain truths. In weeping over the insecurity of suburbanites, they neglect to mention that there

141

are sixty million of us, one third of the nation living their leisure time far from the mother metropolis. In building their image of the suburbanite as a brief-cased neurotic enslaved by train schedules, they've shrugged off the simple count that shows white-collar suburbanites outnumbered by blue-collar suburbanites, ignoring the interchangeability of city and suburb dwellers.

In suggesting that the suburbanite is a coward fleeing the city's problems, they shun the real interpretation—that he is reacting traditionally to the American drive to pioneer new areas, plunging headlong into real, immediate problems such as water supplies, sewers, sensible traffic, roomy classrooms, and police and fire departments. In grieving that suburbanites devote all their spare time to golf and parties, they overlook his schools and churches and hospitals and town halls and community houses. They forget that these things, reflecting so well the character of a nation, were realized by men who spend their days running industrial empires and driving buses and arguing in court and tending the sick and selling neckties and designing buildings and running banks and managing hotels, and who hustle home at night to attend tiresome committee meetings.

To ridicule suburbia is to forget that suburbia is people who have found a more pleasant, more rewarding way of living together—something which has long eluded nations.

I've often wondered how much mileage the movies and TV and novels can get out of the theme that it's somehow asocial to take pleasure in fumeless, grassy, tranquil towns, away from exhaust pipes and smokestacks. I'm amazed that somewhere along the line some magazine editor hasn't penciled out the error that suburban homes are built too close to each other, when in reality the suburbanite has more acreage than the city dweller. It beats me how cliff dwellers who can smell the chops broiling in the neighboring apartment can weep over the suburbanite's lack of privacy. And I always get a jolt when someone tells me that my poor children, far from the cultural and business center, have "no place to explore."

We live thirty miles from Chicago, but my children have been more often than I to the Chicago Museum of Natural History, to the Art Institute of Chicago, to the Adler Planetarium and Astronomical Museum, and to the Shedd Aquarium. Indeed their return visits and what they learn there, against my one expedition, have become downright embarrassing for me. ("I'm going to see Leo Miner tonight, Dad." "Okay. You two going to a movie?")

No place to explore? They're a hundred yards from a lake, where they fish, sail, raft, and skate; where they gaze at ducks resting on their southern flights; where they can watch raccoons plucking frogs from the water by the light of the moon and marvel at the tunneling of muskrats. They're five minutes away from cattle ranches and farms where they can chase rabbits till they run out of salt. They're ten minutes away from the village library and the $1,200,000 Health Museum. They're fifteen minutes away from the venerable Graue Mill where the big water wheel still grinds corn after a hundred and fourteen years, and Old Castle Inn, built in 1836, where Abe Lincoln used to stop. They're twenty minutes away from one of the finest zoos in the Midwest, from a forest preserve where they can camp overnight, and from the eleven-hundred-acre, free-admission Morton Arboretum, where forty-eight hundred different species grow.

And occasionally we take the half-hour drive to the state penitentiary in Joliet, whose high walls have served me well when I've had an especially difficult point to make with Paul.

True, suburban life has made it inconvenient for them to explore the murky saloon fronts in the Loop, and the marquees of Hollywood's "realistic" movies, and the ballooned pictures in front of the strip-tease dens. But you can't have everything.

143

This is not to deny that suburbia spawns problems peculiar to the more leisurely life. I hear complaints from people who have drifted into so many organizations and clubs, they no longer have time to read a book or take a Sunday nap. But almost invariably these complaints come from parents who don't know how to, or are afraid to, say no. And generally they're afraid to say no to their children, who demand expensive cashmere sweaters and calf-leather loafers because two or three in the crowd have them, and membership in the dance class and swim class and drama class and charm class and in the bowling league.

Afraid of being unpopular, some people will join a dog-training club because a friend raves about it, then run out and buy a dog to go with it. Some mothers are bone-weary and guilt-stricken about the grind, but still they run—Monday to the charity tea, Tuesday to the garden club, Wednesday to the PTA meeting, Thursday to the adult-education class, Friday afternoon to the bridge game, Friday night to the den mothers' session, and Saturday to the MacWhoopees for black olives, cheese dip, and highballs. Each of these projects is fine in itself, but in themselves they comprise a social octopus clutching at their time, energy, gasoline tank, nerves, pocketbook, and family schedule. Add to this a husband who runs too, and you'll often find children marked for trouble. Because there isn't a great deal that separates adult negligency from juvenile delinquency. And delinquency doesn't come only in blue jeans and sneakers. It also walks in calf leather and cashmere.

There are some who say it takes a lot of courage to say no in the face of neighbors and friends and the children and the children's friends. I don't think it does, and perhaps this is because in my case saying no has simply been a matter of survival. I mean, a man can buy just so many Girl Guide cookies and that's it. With some regret one Sunday afternoon I said no to the girl with the cookies, and I said no to a local raffle, and I said no to a neighbor canvassing for contributions to help find the cure for a major disease. I just couldn't give any more, and I didn't feel in the least humiliated. Nor do I think that triple-no afternoon cut into our popularity very much.

It's nice to support a sound, worthy cause when a child brings home a five-dollar book of tickets from school or church. But when Paul, Georgia, Shonagh, and Nelda each comes home with a book, I would be a fool to buy all four because I don't want to see the children embarrassed, when I'm overdrawn at the bank. Contrary to what some experts say, I believe that, instead of giving a child a complex, a little embarrassment can do him some good in the long run. I was embarrassed plenty of times as a boy, and I can't say that it turned me against the world.

The first couple of times, Paul was mortified at the prospect of returning his unsold book of tickets and decided to palm them off on the neighborhood. But I forbade that too. If I couldn't support our neighbors' drives, I wasn't going to subject them to ours—especially with a child as clout. So back went the tickets, and the children soon discovered that they lost no face with their teachers or classmates, and there was no dip in their grades.

The suburbanite has to make a stand against conformity somewhere, even if it means earning the pique of a couple of neighbors. I did, because of a dismal neurosis I call stereophobia—I have a dreadful fear of sound amplification as indulged in by stereophonic fans who don't hear so well. When they threw a party I couldn't avoid, I used to sit alone in a corner and sulk, because the script was always the same.

When the party was barely ten minutes old, the host would rise, wet hands a-tremble, a demented gleam shriveling his eyes and his voice changing into a hiss of ecstasy (sometimes froth would appear on the lower lip, but only in extreme cases). Then, with a fluty "Here we go," he would turn on the "equipment," which only a witless clod would call a record player.

So we would sit on the floor (chairs are considered gauche for these sessions), legs akimbo and eyes closed, listening to the "true" sound. Once I cheated and opened my eyes: wall-to-wall yoga in an opium den.

Interrupting these trances with conversation is sacrilegious. If one must leave the room, one raises one's hand, nods knowingly all around, and departs on tiptoe (opening one's eyes in the other room is not only permissible but recommended).

At the last such party—and it *was* the last—I got trapped into an hour and forty minutes of the "true" sounds of the subway. I don't want to seem a sophisticate, but having spent a good deal of time in New York, much of it in the subways, I have what you might call a working knowledge of subway sounds.

But we had to sit through the rattle and the crash. No matter that the walls shook. No matter that one of the goldfish suffered a cardiac and sank to the bottom. No matter that the glass splintered in my hand, hurling beer all over the birdcage.

At this juncture a small chunk of plaster dropped from the ceiling into a plate of cottage cheese reposing on the lap of a large lady on my left. "Excuse me," I whispered, trying not to point, "there's some plaster in——"

Still in a trance, she withered me with one word: "Please . . ." Whereupon she woke up momentarily, speared the piece of plaster, and daintily devoured it.

When it was over, the guests pulled themselves together and the host passed around the stylus—only a peasant would call it a needle—and it went from hand to hand, evoking admiring clucks such as "brilliant diamond work" and "honed in Switzerland, no doubt." Then it came my turn. "Fourteen carats?" I asked, with the nonchalant air of the accomplished boor. With that, the stylus slipped out of my clumsy fingers and into the pan of spaghetti sauce.

There was nothing to do, then, but leave. By subway.

Earlier, at another party, it was airplanes. That record had every imaginable sound associated with planes, including the nervous laughter of devout cowards. *Rrrrrrrrr-wopppp! Eeeeeeeee-frutsz!* and all that. It all could have been bearable, but the ecstatic who hosted the miserable evening lived on the edge of the airport, with planes scraping his shingles every forty seconds and dozens of honest-to-hi-fi *rrrrrrrr-wopppps* and feathered props wheezing and snorting all over his back yard. And amid all this nonsense a four-engine monster glided in about four feet above his clothesline and I ran around throwing up the windows and shouting, "Hey, look! A real one. Let's listen!"

It was as if I had broken into an unhinged giggle at a funeral. And again, of course, I had to leave.

I often run into one other suburban problem for which there's no solution short of germ warfare—the convergence of the neighborhood's little people in our yard. It's nice when your child has three or four pals to play with and fight with and get dirty with and live life to the fullest with. But when you get up there with eight children, the yard begins to look like the playground at the orphanage. I've come home on late afternoons and actually counted twenty-two children running, rolling, and (bless them all) trampling the crab grass into submission.

These daily convocations bring up a multitude of urgent matters: congestion ("Only four on the seesaw at one time; the rest of you get off!"); traffic ("Don't run over the babies with your wagon; go *around* them"); mediation ("Stop pulling down her pants and she'll give you back your turtle"); medical care ("It's not bleeding, and besides, you've already had five Band-Aids this morning"); irrigation ("If you want another drink use the hose, you little sponge"); hearings on

147

appeal ("If you'll give him back his turtle he'll stop pulling down your pants"); penal measures ("And you're to stay out of this yard for three days!"); communications ("You may *not* use the phone; yell at her from here"); health and welfare ("A little sand won't hurt you; finish the sandwich or go home and eat"); community spirit ("Let's all get down on our hands and knees and look for Claude's dental braces"); budgetary vetoes ("I *know* the Good Humor man's here, but I can't buy sixteen Eskimo Pies *every* day"); and internal affairs ("Good grief, you went to the bathroom just five minutes ago!").

Helen isn't the only one burdened with this howling responsibility. Other women oversee yardsful of progeny-at-large, but with an interesting variation: they hang up a shingle that says "Mothers' Helper Haven" or "Nursery Nook," charge twenty dollars a head a week, and retire to the Florida Keys at the age of forty-two. But Helen earns nothing but palpitations, so when she starts looking up the flight schedules to Canada I summon all the little people, sort out our own, order the others to collect their property ("Your left sock's in the mailbox, Cynthia"), pat them gently on the head, and say, "Time to go home. Lisa's coming down with the measles. You got that, now? *Mee-zils.* But tell your mothers not to worry—she'll be all right in a few days."

I'm surprised that what is probably the world's oldest children's game doesn't have a name. I'm sure it originated before dibs or tag, and it was probably first tried out when man devised the split-level cave. For want of a name I call it stay-the-night. Spawned in friendship and nomadism, it consists of staying the night at somebody else's house—a sort of musical beds with homework that helps to still the occasional urge to run away from home and join the circus or the Rockettes.

In small families stay-the-night doesn't present too many

148

problems, but, like kick-the-can, the hazards increase with the number of players. If you have two children, one overnight guest is conspicuous; but with our eight, an extra little girl or two tends to blend into the scenery, as it were, and the expansion can easily go unnoticed—especially if the visitor's parents don't care if the game goes into overtime. When they start calling me Daddy I figure it's time they folded their tent-flap pajamas and silently stole away.

One complication of stay-the-night occurs when the parents haven't been notified or have forgotten that their child will be overnighting elsewhere. Late one night I got home from work after the entire household was asleep and just as the phone started to ring. It was from a lady who wanted to know if her Eunice was with us.

"It's possible," I said. (We had just moved into the neighborhood.) "I'll take a look."

I went to the older girls' room, where I found that not only was Georgia sharing her bed with a stay-the-nighter, but so was Shonagh. On the way back to the kitchen I glanced into another bedroom and discovered that Nelda was playing hostess too. When I got back to the lady on the phone, I said, innocently enough, "Would you describe her for me?"

There was a horrified gasp at the other end of the line.

Once somebody's little Marcella stayed the night from Friday through Sunday morning, and since we couldn't rearrange our own harried schedule to take her home, she toddled off to church with the second shift. When her parents came to fetch her I explained that she was at mass with some of ours.

Her mother's smile was embarrassed, but pleasant. "At mass?" she said. "But we're not Catholic, you know."

"I know that," I said. "But she wanted to go, so I thought it would be all right." (It was too, and Marcella's only complaint as she rubbed her knees was, "At our church we get to sit down more.")

At times the stay-the-nighter will participate in our morning bathroom conferences, and I have to listen to incidental intelligence I'd rather not hear, like, my-daddy-makes-his-own-breakfast-and-he-hates-it-does-yours?, or my-mommy's-teeth-sleep-in-a-cup-on-the-vanity-at-night-why-don't-your-teeth-come out-too?

And when I leave for the train and my brood lines up for the good-by kiss, a puzzled little stay-the-nighter will sometimes snuggle up to the end of the line and pucker up too. You don't need a whole lot of time to interpret a certain wistful look in the eyes of a child.

For a long time I resented turning our yard (and house) into a recreation center. Couldn't I come home just one night when I wouldn't have to get out of the car and clear the carport of scooters and doll houses? And what in blazes were the kids doing with our shuttlecocks? Eating them?

I got tired of putting the questions to Helen, because her answers didn't solve anything. So I turned on the little people themselves in an exasperated moment one day, and let them have it. "Don't you kids have homes? You, there, with my paintbrush in your pocket, do you have to spend all your time here? Couldn't you play in your own yard for a change?"

The boy, a tubby urchin of about six, fumbled in his pocket for the paintbrush. "Yes," he whispered, "I guess so."

"Then why don't you stay there sometimes?"

He leaned over and carefully placed the paintbrush on the grass at his feet, and the small rim of fat under his chin trembled a little as he said, "Because I like to live here."

And then it came over me that their parents weren't sending them over to get rid of them. The children were gravitating to our place simply because here they found more of their kind to talk to and do things with. It wasn't that we had swings, because they had swings too. It wasn't our sand

150

pile, because they had sand piles too. And they had things in their yards we didn't have in ours—wading pools and push-pedal cars, and dogs and cats, and garages crammed with wonderful things to break and lose, and tents, and hamsters, and patios to bounce balls on, and tall, sturdy trees to climb.

And it wasn't that ours were personality kids. It was just that at our place there were eight. And that meant that at least one of them would be around at all times, including naptime.

So we ceased blaming the parents, for it had been a long time since we'd been plagued by the plaint of an only child: "I have nobody to play with."

There are always neighbors who delight in recruiting others for their projects. Once we had one, a bachelor, who seemed to feel that there was something a little abnormal about me because I couldn't get excited over the idea of a garden. His theory was that the suburbanite, deep down, was really gratifying the urge of modern man to return to the soil. The only urge I had in going to the suburbs was to put distance between myself and the city's switchblade set, flooding rivers, maiming automobiles, and odd landlords and landladies. As a side issue, I had discovered that the farther away I got from the city, the closer I got to myself. But my neighbor, a pastoral type whose pockets were always stuffed with seed envelopes, didn't see it that way. He was determined to turn me into a weekend farmer, to the point where he became a pest about it.

"You see things different," he'd say, "when you turn over a shovelful of fresh black soil." All I could see was a fry of wriggly, ugly pink worms, and I tried to tell him so gently, but he would have none of it.

"That corner, there," he mused, "is a natural for tomatoes, and I think we should plant the zucchini over——"

"Zucchini? What's that?"

"It's like squash. What did you think it was?"

"Well, if you must know," I said, "it sounds like somebody that's shot out of a cannon."

"You'll like zucchini," he went on.

"But I don't even like squash," I protested. "Besides, we just don't have the time to——"

"Right by the peas I think a little escarole would be nice," he said, pacing off the area in long, feverish strides.

"I never heard of escarole," I said.

He gave me a patronizing look. "The endive family," he sighed. "Delicious."

This was getting out of hand. "It all sounds very sweet," I said, "but it's not for us. You've got the tomatoes where the swings are, and you're putting the bikini——"

"Zucchini."

"—the zucchini where the sandbox is. And out there where you see peas, that's where the kids are going to play croquet if I ever get a croquet set, and someday I'd like to put a patio where you want to plant your silly endive. And anyway, I don't know the first thing about gardening."

"You get into this," he persisted, "and you'll have a little old green thumb in no time."

At this point I was tempted to thrust my little old thumb, green or no, into his eye. "You don't seem to understand," I said. "I'm just not interested."

He shook his head sadly. I felt as if I'd uttered a blasphemy. "You don't know what you're missing," he said. "It's a wonderful thrill to start with just a little seed and create something, and take care of it and watch it grow."

I looked at Helen, who was standing by, quite pregnant again. "It sure is," I said.

And soon after that, Nelda was born.

Chapter 13

WHEN I'm asked to speak before the journalism class at a school or college, I invariably run into a small embarrassment. When we get to the question period I'm asked how the fledgling goes about getting a newsman's job. I have to tell the students I simply don't know, because 1) I never went to journalism school (except to make speeches), and 2) the ways in which I got my own jobs were too bizarre to recommend.

The day I arrived in Montreal from the mines I moved in with my brother, Vincent, and while unpacking my bag I told him I hoped to get a start on some newspaper. "There are lots of papers in this town," he said, "and there's one just a couple of blocks away. If you look through the window you can see it from here." Sure enough, you could, and Vincent, an impetuous type, suggested we walk over and give it a try. It seemed the thing to do, the place being close by.

A man seldom forgets his first important job, and my remembrance of mine is sharp, because an hour later I was walking out of the editor's office on what seemed to be somebody else's legs. "I don't get it," I told Vincent in the hallway. "I start Monday."

He pushed me into the elevator. "Well, hurry up and let's get out of here," he said, "before they change their mind."

One morning a year later, in the Criminal Courts Building, a news-agency editor substituting for a truant reporter on a short-staff day asked me to direct him to a trial he had to cover. I was covering the same trial, so we sat in on it together. I had never before met the man (though he was familiar with my by-line), yet when we walked into the press-room after court had adjourned for lunch he asked me if I'd like to work for his outfit. I said I would, and then and there he phoned his boss and, after a short chat, told me I'd just been hired. It seemed like a weird, even crude way of doing things, but at that instant the news agency was in the market for a Frenchman who wrote English, and I returned to my office to turn in my story—and my resignation.

The move from United Press to Tulsa had come about through a single letter to Mr. Jones, and the transfer from Tulsa to *Time* had been another rare lump of luck. And it was another letter—again to Mr. Jones—that set our sights on San Francisco.

Almost.

I had written to Mr. Jones that I wanted to leave *Time* to return to newspaper work if I could join, not a newspaper, but a newspaper chain with its spread of opportunities. Mr. Jones must have fallen over himself in going to work on it, because within about a month—I'm amazed to this day at how quickly things are done in this country—I received a letter from the Scripps-Howard command. It invited me to a spring meeting of the chain's nineteen newspapers in Washington, where I would be interviewed by the editor of the San Francisco *News*, and the editor of the Memphis *Commercial-Appeal*. Over the years I had heard nothing but gasps of envy for San Franciscans and their gracious way of life, and at *Time* a transfer to that bureau was considered a plum.

"San Francisco!" I said to Helen. "How lucky can we get?"

When I checked into the hotel in Washington I found that my first interview had been scheduled (alphabetically, perhaps) with Frank Ahlgren of Memphis, an editor so all-out engaging (as was the salary) that I was intrigued with the idea of working for him by the time we lit our second cigarette. "Then it's settled," he said. "No need to see my San Francisco friend down the hall. It's first come, first served."

When I got home I told Helen, "We're not going to San Francisco."

"We're not?" she said.

"No. We're going to Memphis."

"Oh," she said.

What made the greatest impact on us in Memphis, aside from the altogether delightful winters, was the racial problem. As Canadians, we were not accustomed to colored citizens in substantial numbers, and I remember that during my college days in Winnipeg the sight of a Negro on the street was something that caused neck-craning. But in Memphis every third individual was a Negro and, more important, we were there (1953–56) during the Supreme Court's ruling on school desegregation that uncorked the long fermenting unrest.

I had mixed feelings on the matter. I was almost totally ignorant of the historical and social background of the problem, and even when I became acquainted with it, I didn't feel, as an outsider, in a position to judge it impartially. Like a guest caught up in a sudden squabble in the home of friends, I could only look on in dismay as tempers bristled and voices shrilled.

Ours was a peculiar feeling because, as aliens, we found ourselves in the center of an intellectual tug of war—now pulled to the Southern view, now drawn to the Northern stand. Even a foreigner to the region could sense that, despite the smoldering of emotions beneath the surface, there had long been a tranquillity among the people of both colors and at least an outward harmony in the social structure, and now these were no more.

I could not completely share the Northerner's absolute shock at the Southern attitude because I felt that one could not fully understand a regional mood from a distance. One had to become a part of it, and even after being a part of it for three years I was still confused about the emotional hold of long tradition. And I found most distressing the almost complete lack of Negro leadership at the local level (at that time) in church, in politics, and in labor and the professional worlds. It seemed unfortunate that the rallying cry should be sounded from the faraway bastions to the north, and that counsel and direction should come almost solely from the monthly visits of New York delegations, in for an afternoon of fiery speeches and fund collections and out again by nightfall. Nowhere in the South, in those three years, was I able to detect Negro leadership of substance among adults (it arose mostly from the teen-agers, near the turn of the decade). Even more deplorable was the fact that the two fellowships which the Negro believed to be his stanch friends, the labor unions and his church, failed him dismally.

Though the vast majority of the nation's Negroes are members of various Protestant denominations, their church—in the North as well as in the South—seemed lamentably silent and inert. This was my feeling when we were there, and as late as 1961 the Reverend Dr. Robert J. McCracken, pastor of New York's Riverside Church, felt there had been no improvement.

"Segregation is more pronounced and more entrenched in the Protestant churches of America," he wrote, "than in any other of our social institutions. So far from hastening integration, they are hindering it. North and South, we are saying one thing and doing another."

It has also been difficult for me to reconcile the pious pronouncements of solidarity from the labor unions with their actions. A. Philip Randolph, the only Negro on the executive council of the AFL-CIO (which collects dues from 1,100,000 Negroes), was moved to say (in 1960): "Negro citizens are second-class citizens in the labor movement today. The fact is, racial discrimination and segregation in the labor movement are taken for granted. They are viewed with utter complacency, if not indifference."

As a Catholic, I kept waiting for some sign, some voice from my church in Memphis, but little came. Yet as I recalled my Jesuit education and, indeed, the elementary principles of childhood catechism, the position of the Catholic seemed axiomatic and incontestable: if all men derive from the same first parents, Adam and Eve, and are redeemed by the same Christ, then to deny all men the same dignity is inherently immoral. Since my church teaches that in the eyes of God there is no fundamental difference between the races, then discrimination is intrinsically sinful.

The very definition of Catholicism clearly embraces the element of universality. For a Catholic to practice discrimination was to me the rebuff of an essential precept of doctrine.

As a Canadian and a Catholic I found the standoff perplexing. And I found it sad, because the Southern people were by nature friendly, hospitable, and well intentioned. But it was ominously obvious that a storm was approaching, and I knew that someday my children would be asking me questions I would find difficult to answer. Gradually I began to feel that it would be better for them to be away from the scene of the dying throes of traditions they did not share and would never understand. So when the Chicago opportunity at the *Sun-Times* presented itself, I decided to take it with quiet relief. Perhaps this was running away from turmoil, a form of cowardice. But I was, after all, only a guest. And at least until I became a citizen, there seemed to be no contribution for good that I could make.

At this point, the oddity attending the way I found jobs came full circle. I had confided my feelings to a close friend, Harold Krelstein, the president of Plough Broadcasting Company, who lives in Memphis. We were leaving the dining room of the Peabody Hotel one day when he said, "Marshall Field is a friend of mine. I'll be in Chicago tomorrow, and I'm going to tell him about you." As we passed the news counter he picked up the *Sun-Times* and gave it to me. "Here's your homework," he said. "That's where you're going."

About three weeks later I received a letter from Marshall Field, Jr., publisher of the Chicago *Sun-Times* and the Chicago *Daily News*, inviting me to visit him, at his expense, to discuss a job.

Marcia had come to us in Memphis, and with five children I couldn't pass up the salary offered me by the Chicago *Sun-Times*.

As one who now has ten mouths to feed, I look at the financial section of the newspaper with something less than ecstasy. There isn't much reason for me to follow the market, even if I had time to translate all those columns of quotations into French. Because the only shares I own is that clump of stock in Paul Molloy Associates, a decidedly non-profit organization partnered by Helen and me and the eight children (as co-chairman of the board, Helen and I each control forty-six per cent, and the remaining eight per cent is held evenly by the eight junior partners).

But not long ago I was intrigued by a financial-page story about an electronic computer that apparently takes a dim view of parenthood. Developed by a Chicago consultant, this thought monster digests gossip about your personal life on a card and totes up your score as a credit risk. (Compassion doesn't count; there's no blank on the card for that.)

For example, if you're married, you get one point, and you get another if you own your own home. If you're a childless couple, the machine figures you have extra money to spend, so it gives you another credit point. But if you rent you lose a point, and right there that cancels out apartment-dwelling newlyweds into neutrals, until they hurry up and get pregnant and win another minus point.

I think the computer advocates birth control, because I understand that when you get up to three children the little wheels inside go *wrupp-wrupp*—which is electronic language for tsk-tsk. I can't prove this, but I suspect that the warning light ("Stop, you fool") goes on at four children. I say that because I called the man who created the computer (it's used extensively by credit managers in Chicago) and he told me that a man with five children starts right off as a minus because he's always broke. If you accept that assumption— and the man with the machine told me it's accepted as official when your credit status is drawn up—the computer can do little when you feed it a card that says six children but recite the Sermon on the Mount ("Blessed are the poor," etc.). If you have seven children, I suppose it simply swallows hard and plays a recording of "Nobody Knows the Trouble I've Seen." Obviously there would be little point in giving it a go at my card. I know very well it would promptly make vulgar, clanking noises, blow a pair of fuses, light up the panel like a penny arcade, and spit back my card with the stamped-in-red legend: "Follow That Man!"

I resent that machine's thinking, because it won't compromise. I have a friend, an assistant bottle capper in a goat's-milk dairy, who for years lived in a borrowed trailer on the banks of a nameless creek on Chicago's South Side. Not long ago, because he was sober and industrious and his brother died and left him the company, he became the two-hundred-thousand-dollar-a-year head of a chain of restaurants and moved into a palatial home. A good credit risk? No-ooo, said the computer, because he had just switched jobs and hadn't been a home owner for more than a month.

Despite my score—I'm not sure what it is, because the computer didn't function below minus sixty—I haven't had too much trouble with my credit. Each month I try to send my creditors something, even if it's just a note to advise that, yes indeed, things are coming along well (everything considered) and how nice of them to ask, and to report that, bad luck, my assets are as miserable this month as last but next month might produce a contribution, like possibly five dollars. I've found that a stamp and the truth seldom evoke severe rebuke.

But I think I'm able to stumble along on credit because of my contacts. The fact that the Prudential Insurance Company has a deep, abiding interest in our house has proved of immense value. Most of my creditors seem to feel that the company shows promise of amounting to something. And I believe my contact with the nine dependents is a help rather than a hindrance; because, confound it, how do you skip town with a mob like that? Where do you hide?

I'm more fortunate than most in that I have interesting collateral. Dr. Robert Krvavica, my dentist, is entrusted with the care of our three hundred teeth (give or take a few that haven't arrived or have departed forever). I've always owed him plenty, but I don't think he's insecure about it, because he owns all rights to those three hundred X ray plates. (Certainly they're useful. He could paper his study with them and have the quaintest conversation piece in town.) And for baby-blessed fathers like me the best time of the year is spring, after income-tax time. Asked for collateral, I'm able to report that the United States government owes *me* money. That's always hard to top.

But I got sidetracked; what I wanted to say was that it's getting rough on full-house fathers when computers get into the act of panning papahood. Over the years, television has done a deft job of picturing the father as a bumbling hammerhead unable to find his way out of the supermarket; now we have the aluminum accountant that can digest decimals and vomit his credit rating. And, heavens to high chairs, agitating nearby are the professional bleeding hearts who prate that fecundity is some sort of pox.

I can't remember if it was a fit of laughter or of pique, but a fit of something made me hang on to the statements of two prominent economists who lectured within a fortnight of each other in Chicago. One of them was Demographer Ansley Coale, director of population research at Princeton University, who tut-tutted: "In today's trend toward larger families, children are popular—like tail fins on cars. Perhaps small families worry that their neighbors will think they can't afford to have more children." Well, now, there were no tail fins on cars when we started on our nine, and I keep wondering if I wasn't somehow ahead of my time. But that isn't likely, because Bach was one of twenty children, and Ben Franklin was one of seventeen, and Tennsyon was one of twelve, as was Beethoven, and Washington Irving was one of eleven, and so on. I sometimes wonder if children were popular then like the fringe on top of surreys.

The other economist was Dr. Lee Rainwater, director of special studies at Chicago's Social Research, Incorporated, who delivered this conclusion: "Large families are symbols of the father's ability to provide, and evidence of his virility. Since he feels weak and ineffective in relation to the outside world, a large family represents a kind of defiant demonstration that he is a real man."

Well, let that be a lesson to me. And let it be a lesson to other fathers of nine children, like, say, Joseph P. Kennedy who needed another symbol of his ability to provide (apart from that hundred million dollars), and managed to conquer his ineffectiveness "in relation to the outside world" by co-producing the President of the United States and (possibly as an afterthought) the nation's Attorney General.

As a fairly new nephew, I'm not about to tell Uncle Sam how he should run his house, but it's hard to conceal a certain admiration for the prestige which France accords the prolific parent, by law. When a woman becomes pregnant over there, the government rewards the successful *amourette* with a sixty-dollar grant. When the child is born, the couple receives a bonus of eighty dollars, and it gets better, for the father, from there on in. The government decrees that he may take three weekdays off with pay, giving him all the time he needs to recover his senses, register the child, and toast the event with his friends. This last he presumably does with the eighty-dollar bonus, which buys a lot of cigars and muscatel. And for the next eighteen years that child will bring him a monthly allowance of fifteen dollars.

The windfall swirls merrily on with succeeding pregnancies. With three children (or more) he becomes entitled to a pension of fifty dollars (or more) a month and a special "large family" card, which may explain why Frenchmen are such great lovers: this card entitles him to half fare on buses, subways, and trains, and a five- to ten-per-cent mark-off in certain department stores (with six or more children, it's seventy-five per cent off on public transportation and *au diable la bicyclette*). The benefits cease when the child is eighteen and drafted for military service, except for the father of six (or more) children: he gets a new card that entitles him to a thirty-per-cent reduction on transportation for the rest of his life. The mother gets nothing but morning sickness, the government choosing to lavish its gratitude on her mate for his role in triggering the population explosion.

My interest in this matter isn't one of envy, because government grants in the form of a baby bonus leave me cold, since they're merely a partial refund on taxes. I cite it to suggest that when the worldwide birth-control forces move into France, they'll likely find that fifty million Frenchmen can't be wrung from their resolve to abide by the Creator's master plan.

I probably wouldn't get exercised over all this if the professional campaigners for birth control didn't make me feel so much like a social outcast, a sexually ignorant pariah with no order to his life. Everywhere I turn these days I run into the apostles of contraception—on radio panels and TV documentaries, in the newspapers and magazines, on the public forum and in the mailbox (it's depressing to read a letter that starts off, cordially enough, with "Dear Friend," and then to discover in the last paragraph that some of us careless oafs are impregnating ourselves into extinction. Makes you feel you've slipped up somewhere as a citizen).

I don't know why this should be, because we fathers of large families are anything but shirkers. We pay our cigarette and gasoline taxes; we support schools and churches (and we do pretty well by the hospitals too); for the most part, we don't clutter up traffic in the corridors of divorce and juvenile courts; and we're the worst enemy a recession ever had: we make solid contributions toward the standard of living of pediatricians, shoe salesmen, barbers, baby photographers, butchers, general practitioners, bassinette designers, grocery clerks, and drugstore owners.

We contribute to the economy of many industries—cotton, dairy, bubble-gum, Band-Aid, nipple, soap, toy, Kool-Aid, toothpaste, safety-pin, soda-cracker, and dozens of others. (At our house a roll of bathroom tissue lasts about as long as a roll of film in Yellowstone Park.) In addition, the kumquat and pickle distributors owe a lot to our wives.

But still the crusade rolls on toward the prevention of births, unmindful that the marriage age is descending and the family size ascending (between 1950 and 1960 in this country the average family went from 3.54 to 3.68 persons); unmindful that many people reject artificial contraception as immoral, not by some church law affecting one religious segment, but by divine law binding on the whole human race. (As a Catholic, I'm sometimes asked if we are not directed to have all the children physically possible, which would give us exactly nineteen at this point. I have to explain

163

that this is not so, but that if the marriage rights are used they must not be artificially frustrated.)

Before this thing gets out of hand, before we take to sneaking down back alleys and farming out part of the progeny, I think we fathers of large families should organize into some kind of group to set the record straight. I don't know what we'd call it, but Masterplanned Parenthood Association might be all right. There would be no dues, because most members, being broke, would want credit, and we know what the computer says about that. And there would be no formal meetings, because, what with one pregnancy after another, we're all a little pressed for time. But we would have a purpose: each in his own way could serve as a sort of "truth squad" in the wake of the birth controligarchy.

Our first objective, I think, would be to put to rest the canard that we're disastrous. This was the indictment made across the land by Sir Julian Huxley during a nationwide tour. Britain's Sir Julian led the forces that presented a petition to the U.N., urging it to undertake a worldwide program for birth control. "International birth control," he said, "is needed on a large scale and as soon as possible to avert the eventual disaster of starvation and misery."

Members of the Masterplanned Parenthood Association will hear this threat of disaster quoted at parties and around the water cooler by friends who may be horrified that the population is growing at an annual rate of 1.6 per cent. They should accept the statistic, then gently remind their friends that Huxley and his group have a regrettable habit of leaving two other statistics in their pocket: the world's food production is growing at an annual rate of 2.7 per cent, and industrial production is growing at an annual rate of 4.1 per cent.

When Sir Julian says that uncontrolled contraception "reduces the possibilities of enjoyment of the world's variety and beauty," members should quietly suggest that self-pampering

164

and material luxuries are not all there is to human happiness. They should point out that there are other values, and, if pressed to cite one, they might refer to the helping of underdeveloped countries by nations consistently blessed with a surplus.

Nor should members be unnerved by Sir Julian's promise that ending human congestion through birth control will "contribute to better happiness." They should comment softly that if the world's entire population (two and three quarter billions) should be placed in the United States, this country would have the same congestion as now exists in The Netherlands, where, at last word, the people seemed reasonably happy.

If the discussion should get lively, members might counter with a scientist of their own—Demographer-Economist Colin Clark of Oxford University—who says that with commonsense development and production the world can accommodate about sixty billion people comfortably. If this knocks the opponent off balance, members should follow through with Sir Julian's theory of "better happiness," questioning whether telling a couple they mustn't have the number of children they want doesn't approximate a restriction of human happiness.

Birth-control forces have returned from underdeveloped countries and deplored the hunger of large populations. But they have failed to mention the lag in agricultural and technical techniques, and in production and communication (in some countries superstitious taboos allow the destruction of crops by sacred cows and other revered animals). Members of our group should know that this oversight has been rectified by the national business weekly, *Barron's*, which says:

"Wherever famine or misery or the threat thereof exists today in the world, the fault lies not with unplanned families, but with misguided economic policy. The cure, in turn, must be sought not in some kind of pseudo-scientific crusade, but in the more efficient and sensible use of material resources. . . . The crying need in the world is not for fewer lives; it is for more opportunities to make a living."

Members should also take note that when India's Prime Minister Nehru was visited by delegates from the Planned Parenthood Association (not to be confused with the Masterplanned Parenthood Association), he told them that the vast majority of India's peasants believe that children are a gift of God, and that anyone who interferes with childbirth is defying God's will.

Our association's "truth squad" may be chided for disliking Sir Julian because of his public disavowal of the existence of God. Its stand should be that it merely questions his authority as an expert on human relationships. It would not be improper for a member to wonder if an evolutionist is the happiest choice to testify on the intimate rights of married couples, since the desire for parenthood and its fulfillment spring from the natural love of children, the love that binds a man to a woman for life, and the love both have for God.

I have the feeling that there is a place in modern society for a group such as the Masterplanned Parenthood Association. We parents of large families may not be experts on the alleged evolution of man from monkey, but we do know a thing or two (or ten) on how to cope with congestion, and we've found that doing so can, to use Sir Julian's words, "contribute to better happiness."

It would be foolish to deny the problems and hardships of a large family. I once was bitter about them, especially when the flood hit us at the height of Helen's pregnancy and with Georgia in the hospital, but time has a way of teaching us that they don't make troubles any more like they used to. As I write this, I'm terribly overdrawn at the bank, but when I'm tempted to feel sorry for myself over it I need only walk out the house to look at the zigzag of shadows that hover above the neighboring housetops.

Because within walking distance is the house where the boy who was Lisa's age drowned last summer; and the house where the teacher, the one who told the funniest stories at our parties, was killed in his car two summers ago; and the house where there can be no more children; and the house with the child whose mind will never reach the age of reason; and the house where divorce removed the mother; and the house where the boy who played Little League baseball with Paul died three months after they found the cancer in his chest.

And I look from all that to my own house, where there hasn't even been a need for braces on the teeth, and I think of the warmth of being loved by one alone, and I know that in that house I am loved by nine, and nine myself I love, so that in my house, so near the houses of shadows, there are ninety love affairs going on around the clock.

But there are times when it gets so noisy you wonder if your nerves will hold out. One Sunday afternoon I was wondering where I could possibly escape, when a ring on the telephone added to the bedlam. It was from Joe E. Brown. "I've heard about your children," he said, "and I was wondering if I could whiz by for a minute to see them." No press agents or photographers or other gimmicks (this is the first time the incident sees print)—just a man who never forgot what the long laughter of children, and their noise, had done for him.

The minute stretched into hours, during which he spellbound the children with the story of what he was doing at Paul's age: swinging from a trapeze under the Ringling tent in San Francisco, until the earthquake put a stop to that.

When I asked him to pose for a home-movie clip he not only turned handsprings on the lawn, he recreated his classic windup routine from "Alibi Ike." When it was over, Nelda, by now madly in love with him, asked, "Will you come again to see us?"

"Of course I will," he said. Then, drenched in perspiration, his clothes in disarray, and his hair falling over his glasses, he slid into his rented car and drove the thirty miles back to his Chicago hotel.

At about the same hour the following Sunday—this time unannounced—he was at the door again. "I thought I'd come back and look at that movie of ours," he said in that oh-shucks voice of his. He had a two-week stand in "Father of the Bride" with two Sundays off, and that was how he chose to spend them. Toward the end, as Brown was giving him the bottle, Mark had an unfortunate lapse of good manners which left a damper on his lap, and as the childish scramble for his attention increased its pitch, I said, "Doesn't all this noise get on your nerves?"

He grew serious, almost annoyed. "Noise?" he said. "This is music. You've got eight. There were seven kids in our family, and we were poor, and we had the kind of trouble that was always going to be the death of my mother. But I'm sixty-nine years old and she's still going strong, and it isn't the troubles I remember—just the happy noise."

That night at bedtime Nelda came barefooting out of the bathroom with a gory mouthful of that striped toothpaste, and announced that she was engaging herself to Brown. "I hope Father Henehan [our pastor] doesn't mind," she said as an afterthought. "I was going to marry him."

"But Nelda," I said, "Mr. Brown is too old for you."

"He's not so old," she said. "He can stand on his head." Then she nipped some of the saliva off her chin and frowned. "Father Henehan never stands on his head."

Speaking of Brown, people often wonder if the children are impressed with the celebrities in whose circles I move. Not really.

168

I don't do it any more, but there was a time when I might mention that I had been with some interesting personality, but it seldom sparked much excitement. I'd wait for a pause in the dinnertime babble and say, "Guess who I had lunch with today?"

I rarely found any takers, so I'd go right on and say that I had lunched with some performer whose name they'd likely know. Generally the reaction would be a request to pass the catsup or a reminder that I was behind on allowances. I like the childish concept of celebrities; our street is full of them.

There's Mr. Panzica, across the street, who manages a Pony League team and who can play the accordion; he's a celebrity. And there's Mr. Ege, also across the street, who has the large plastic swimming pool; he's another. And there's Mr. Smith next door, who can fix our washing machine in no time at all (not only that, he doesn't remove the lights from his Christmas tree outside until February). And Mr. Starkweather, who lets them play on his Slip-n-Slide.

And there's Dr. Sullivan, who means it when he says it isn't going to hurt. And long-legged Mr. Wright, a veritable gazelle on the softball field. And Mr. Clarke, who lets them stage their plays in his yard (chilrin; 2¢, parints, 5¢). And Mr. Syrett, who has the rowboat, and Mrs. Harnstrom, who has the only hammock on the block. These are the celebrities.

For Georgia, Shonagh, and Nelda the school-time celebrities are the Sisters of St. Joseph at St. Isaac Jogues School. If I should mention that I've just run into Sister Superior on the street, I'm overwhelmed with questions: What did she say? And what did you say? Then what did *she* say to that? Did she talk about my spelling? Didn't she tell you my essay's hanging on the wall? Their feeling toward the teaching sisters runs close to hero-worship, and I think this reflects what I suggested some pages back—that discipline is not only something that children need; it's also something they want.

With six of the eight coming-up girls whose education is entrusted to nuns, I've wondered if one or more might eventually join a religious order. I've also been concerned with my father-of-the-bride obligations: the prospect of what six weddings would cost me in coming years is something that makes me bite my lip, pondering the only two avenues of escape: a mass elopement, or a get-thee-to-a-nunnery hint.

Georgia hopes to become a nun. Shonagh, who's currently stagestruck, is torn between Wagnerian opera and baton twirling. Nelda is firm about growing up to marry Joe E. Brown, whose old movies she adores on television, but, on the other hand, she might just become a nun if something is done about modifying the wimple. ("It's dangerous crossing the street; they can't see the cars.")

On occasions these leanings have evoked clucks of sympathy from people who fear we'd be abandoning the girls to a sort of cloistered vegetality. They seem unaware that it takes a heroic blend of spunk and sacrifice to dedicate one's life to classrooms, bedsores, and missions. If none of the children takes the holy orders, we won't be disappointed; if any receives a vocation, we shall be proud. Very few families are so honored.

Paul has always been more interested in sports stars than celebrities of show business, but a sad experience strengthened this preference, and with it a durable actor lost him as an admirer.

Hinsdale has a summer theater, and the natives are accustomed to seeing stage and screen figures strolling around the village and popping into stores. One Saturday after Paul had helped me with errands, we stopped into the restaurant for a hamburger. As we were leaving he noticed the actor, whom he knew from a TV series, eating alone at a nearby table.

"Do you think he'd mind," Paul asked, "if I went and told him I like his show?" (This was his precise request; of the many theatrical folks he's met, he has never asked for an autograph.)

"Go ahead," I said, "I think he'll like it."

When Paul got to the table, the actor gave him a stony stare. "I never give autographs," he harrumphed, "while I'm eating." With that he plopped a generous forkful of poached egg into his mouth. Paul looked at me, then shifted from one leg to the other.

"But I just wanted to——"

The performer cut him off, this time in a voice heard clearly above the café clatter. "You're interrupting my lunch. Now run along!"

It seemed to take Paul an hour to limp, dragging the hurt behind him, back to the cashier's booth, where I was waiting. I soothed his embarrassment by explaining that since summer-stock players worked under the strain of travel, they were pushovers for small irritations.

The following Saturday we had barely ordered the hamburger when to the table came, this time wearing open-toed sandals and a grin from ear to there, last week's angry actor. With him, and all but holding his hand, was a press agent whom I knew.

"As soon as I spotted you," the publicist said, "my tiger here wanted to meet you."

"I read you all the time, Mr. Milroy," the actor lied. "Delightful column."

The press agent pulled back the chairs facing us, and as the actor sat down he smiled and said, "I hope we're not interrupting your lunch."

"Not at all," I said. Then I could resist it no longer. "By the way, this is my son. I believe he interrupted yours last week."

They didn't stay long.

Few things are more important to Paul than baseball, and his spring training starts Christmas week, when he works on

171

his batting stance in four inches of snow. If I tell him some cowboy star called on me at the office, he yawns; but if I mention running into Bill Veeck in a restaurant, I've justified my existence as columnist. Because Paul knows that interest in baseball didn't come instinctively to me; like most Canadians, I was weaned on hockey, and, in our phlegmatic way, we always managed to control our zeal about it until the play-offs at the close of winter.

After coming to this country I would listen to Americans arguing about batting averages in March, and marvel at the idiocy of it all when the World Series didn't come off till October. Then Paul came home one day to announce that he was joining something called Little League and two months later I had discovered that besides the Rangers, New York also had the Yankees, and the adventures of Detroit's Tigers were more exciting than those of the Red Wings. And I caught the fever, and now I'm a Pony League vice-president.

At one point, life held only three ecstasies for Paul; meeting Casey Stengel, discussing the choke-up with Ernie Banks, and seeing the legendary Ted Williams in action. Two of these thrills had been fulfilled and the third became a reality one night in June when the Boston Red Sox came to Chicago for a weekend wrangle with the White Sox. I, too, had never seen Williams, and with twilight closing in on his career, we would have to see him now or never. So we went to Comiskey Park, where that night Williams did indeed walk in brilliance.

After the game it took us an agonizing time to crawl from the parking lot to the intersection beyond the main gate of the park. But Paul wasn't in any rush to break out of traffic. He settled back, satisfied and tingling, and for a few minutes it was like a litany. "Now I've seen Ted Williams play," he repeated, speaking to the sticky black night. Then from the sultry whirlpool of thirty-five thousand bodies there strode on slender legs a tall, almost scrawny man in an open shirt. "I can't get a cab," he said, his head in the window. "Could I ride to the Loop with you?"

There was an air of cleanliness, about him and he looked honest, so I opened the door and let him in. We rolled in silence for a block, and the finger of coincidence touched the back of Paul's neck with a sudden quiver, and he turned to me and made the words with his mouth: "It's Ted Williams . . ."

Luck had laughed at unbelievable odds.

And for thirty minutes the boy and the man talked out the most important thing in their lives. "Yes . . . I'm forty-one now and it's twenty-five years they've been paying me to play baseball. . . . I won't tell you the corny things, but it's important that I don't smoke and I don't drink, because you'll either be a great athlete or a bum athlete, and you'll just be what you want to be. . . . The one big thing that made it possible? You'll laugh. It's not diet or pills or the constant practice. It's knowing when to rest. I don't care where I am or who I'm with. When I'm tired I go to bed, and it's usually before midnight."

Were there, Paul wondered, any pitchers who really gave him the willies?

"Only one. There's only one that really bothers me—Billy Pierce."

What about that odd wriggle of the hips at the plate? Didn't that hurt the body balance?

"Only one thing is important at the plate—stand up close and don't back up an inch. What you look like isn't important. It's what happens when you hit it."

And then he didn't want to talk baseball any more, or whether he would cap his career as a manager ("an awful, thankless job"), but there were just enough unfinished thoughts to suggest that he would never quit something that, a quarter century ago, had made him blurt, "I want to be an immortal."

His green eyes came to life again. "Baseball isn't that important. You know what's important? This country, and keeping it strong and great. That's important."

Then we were in the Loop and he was gone, and Paul's eyes followed him until the restless lights no longer showed his square shoulders and the bounding stride. "They won't believe me," Paul said softly. "The kids will think I made it up."

Chapter 14

"One, two, a baby is born——
"One, two, a baby is born——
"One, two, a baby——"

AND so it went in rapid monotone, Shonagh's obbligato for rolling rubber as the car chugged northward to Chicago. Shonagh had been deeply impressed by an incidental in the story of the Creation: "Every two seconds [one, two, just like that] somewhere in the world someone is born." And in a lively little corner of her mind it had turned to singsong doggerel which, now that we were far from Memphis and on the road, was starting to rustle my nerves.

I was a little disturbed because we were mightily pregnant again, about eight and a half months' worth, and the doctor in Memphis had made it clear that driving the five hundred and forty miles to Hinsdale at this time involved a risk. "You should be all right," he said, "but this is cutting it pretty thin. I don't think it's a good idea."

I didn't think it was a good idea either, but Helen was determined to make the move. I had been on the job at the *Sun-Times* in Chicago for nearly two months, during which period I'd found the Hinsdale prefab and Helen had found a buyer for the house in Memphis; she was as insistent as she was *enceinte* about getting our show on the road, and, after Patricia, Paul, Georgia, Shonagh, Nelda, and Marcia, she seemed disquietingly serene about the whole thing. True, she had been a mother six times, but I'd never been a midwife, and the prospect of delivering a baby in a cotton patch

175

somewhere, and me unable to pull a splinter without flinching, wasn't at all comfortable.

I couldn't banish from my mind the story told me by a schoolteacher of reputable character who claimed that her aunt had given birth to her first baby one morning after breakfast without being aware of it. Her aunt was still in her nightgown, by the washing machine, when, quite by surprise, a baby boy was born. "She didn't know about it," my friend said, "until she heard the bump on the floor."

I couldn't believe it. I didn't want to believe it, but the schoolteacher wasn't given to exaggeration, and I kept thinking about her aunt and the washing machine and the thud on the floor as we jogged along the highway that September afternoon. I had heard of deliveries attended by policemen and cab drivers, and I had a vague idea that the thing to do was cut and tie the umbilical cord and keep the mother and baby warm. Accordingly, I put a couple of blankets in the trunk of the car and—Helen ignorant of it all—stashed a pair of scissors and a strand of string about four feet long in my pocket. Primitive as it was, the equipment perked up my morale, and I kept sneaking sidelong glances to my right to make sure that nothing was happening.

I can't say that nothing was happening, because—confound it—Helen was carrying an active little creature and I could see the arcing swell of a kicking foot or twitching arm moving jerkily along her stomach. I felt reasonably safe at the approaches to a town, and along the main street I'd even get a little cocky about it, secure in the knowledge that we were only minutes from some hospital. It was between towns that my courage would fade, and on one of these lonely stretches of unpeopled prairie it hit me abruptly—a cramp-like throb in the pit of the stomach, and then my left leg started a crazy jiggle, and hot flashes raced down my arms, and my hands were wet at the wheel. *Which end of the umbilical cord should I knot?*

Much later, Dr. Sullivan was to tell me how foolish that terror was, but at the time I was only aware that one knot was to be tied, and I couldn't decide whether it belonged on the baby's or the mother's side of the cord. I only remember now that, in panic, I figured I had enough string for two knots and, to play it safe, two knots it would be.

But nothing happened that day or that night in the motel or the next morning, and we rolled up to the front of the house in Hinsdale in a blinding rain on a sullen-sky Saturday noon, and I remember how funny we thought it was that just as the car stopped, the air whistled out of the front left tire. Waiting for us in the cab of his moving van was the driver who had carted our possessions from Memphis. He too was sullen, and so was his driving mate; they had been parked there since early morning, and they were damp and weary.

"There's a two-hundred-dollar balance," said the driver, handing me a soggy piece of paper.

"Right," I said, pocketing the bill. "Now let's open up this thing and get the stuff in the house."

"I got to collect," he said, looking down from his cab.

"Don't worry about it," I said. "I arranged all that with your office in Memphis."

"I don't know nothin' about arrangements," he drawled. "This truck's got to stay closed till I collect."

With an initial payment in Memphis, I'd been given a breather on the balance, but evidently there had been some slip-up in paperwork, and the driver refused to open the van doors. Helen was standing in the empty house, looking through the picture window at the ungrassed yard of mud washing away in the pelting rain; and now the exhaustion of the trip, and the long wait for the baby, and the dirty wetness, and the flat tire, and the van that wouldn't open, closed in on her, and she just cried. And the children had no place to sit or lean, so they cried too.

"For God's sake," I told the driver, "find a phone somewhere and get this straightened out *now!* I want that van opened!"

"Nobody in the office Saturday afternoons," he said.

I had ninety dollars to our name, and the next pay check was six days away.

At this point there splashed into view two more candidates for my WILAA (what-I-like-about-America) list, in the person of Mr. and Mrs. Ken Holmgren, from across the street, and Len Hilts, who lived around the bend. Mrs. Holmgren delivered a couple dozen sandwiches, milk, and coffee to Helen, then her husband set about fixing our flat. And standing there with the rain running down our necks, Hilts and I found a mutual, soggy bond: like me, he was a writer; like me, he had five children; like me, he was awaiting a sixth; like me, he had moved around the country; and, like me, he knew the scarcity of cash.

"We've got ten minutes before the bank closes," he said. "Let's go get some."

We raced to the First National Bank, in the heart of Hinsdale, where Hilts pushed me up to the vice-president, Hal Klein. "Look what I found in the rain," he said. "He's got to raise two hundred dollars in a hurry or his mob sleeps with my mob tonight, and that's murder." To my amazement, Klein okayed the loan before we'd stopped dripping. I was so stunned, I couldn't put the money in my pocket. "Don't you want to hear more about me?" I asked.

"When a guy gets stuck with a locked van," he said, "I've heard enough. Go get those doors opened."

I don't think banks need any help from me on their public relations, but I cite the manner of the Hinsdale loan as one of two incidents that punctured—for me, at least— the myth that the cornerstones of banks are fashioned from the hearts of vice-presidents. The other example took place in Memphis where, still tasting the brief thrill of home ownership in Winnipeg, we hankered to buy another one.

On a nervy impulse one morning I walked into the National Bank of Commerce and asked the vice-president, Bill Scott, if he could lend me the amount of a down payment. This despite the facts that:

I had been in Memphis only a few months;
I had no income but a weekly pay check;
I was still an alien;
I didn't have a dollar in his or any other bank;
I had no collateral, not even a car, and
I didn't know a soul in the United States I dared ask to sign the note.

"All I can put up," I told Scott, "is my job and a letter that guarantees me a cosigner."

"Who?" Scott asked.

"Gerhard Kennedy. That's my wife's brother."

Scott picked up the phone. "Where can I reach him?"

"He lives in Calgary."

Scott replaced the phone. "It'll take some talking," he said, in a crashing understatement. "But I'll bring it up at the next board meeting."

Three weeks later we were home owners.

Three hours after Hilts hustled me out of Klein's office we were Hinsdale home owners, with chairs to sit on and beds to sleep in, and that big bully of a van was lumbering away, empty and forgotten.

And three days later Lisa arrived.

We were just becoming accustomed to having a crib in our bedroom again—it fitted fine, except you had to climb over the bed to get to the clothes closet—and at predawn feeding time one day I told Helen, "Just think, in a little while she'll be going through the night and we'll be back to normal again."

Helen patted a soft belch out of Lisa and yawned. "And in just a little while I think we'll be starting all over again."

I wished she wouldn't start rumors like that. Not at four o'clock in the morning.

But by the end of the week Helen confirmed the rumor, and now it was obvious that we would have to add a room. There was plenty of space in the back yard, and we thought about it for a few months and decided that something about twenty feet by ten was what we needed, because when you counted . . .

But Barbara arrived while we were squinting over diagrams, and we figured we'd better make the room a little larger, and we thought and thought some more, until twenty-five feet by twelve looked about right, since we would have to put Paul over here, and Shonagh and Georgia over there, and in the new room we could pile Nelda and Marcia and Lisa and Barbara if we . . .

And ten months after Barbara, on that Christmas morning, Mark arrived, and when the last nail had been hammered into the last slat, the room—it was the dormitory now—went thirty feet in one direction and sixteen in the other.

It had cost forty-six hundred dollars, and while I'd been tempted to press my luck with the banks, I didn't. It had occurred to me that the house was as much Prudential's as it was mine (it was mostly theirs, if I came right down to it, which I did every night of those long pregnancy months), hence they should have a financial stake in any expansion. Why couldn't they put up the building cost, tear up the mortgage, and start all over again with a new, larger mortgage? Why not? said Prudential. And that was that.

My house payments now were larger, but I had my study, a private sanctum in which to write and meditate and just hide in solitary peace. So I bought a desk, a monstrous thing of olden times, and the room between the dormitory and Paul's room became my study; even without a window, it was as nice a luxury as any man could wish for.

It ceased being nice on the fourth day, when we put in

the small table so that Paul, Georgia, Shonagh, and Nelda could have a place to do their homework. And it ceased being a luxury before the week was out, when the little ones moved in with their coffee cans crammed to the brim with crayons.

So the table, handmade for Helen's father forty-five years ago by Indians in the Canadian north, serves as culture and study center for the throng. It eventually became the only practical spot for the record player; and eventually I had to find another place for my scrapbooks, to make room for the schoolbooks; and eventually the schoolbooks had to go else-where, to make room for the coloring books; and eventually my scrapbooks and typewriter and reference stuff lost their nook in the little closet near the table because the mop moved in; then the ironing board moved in; then the vacuum cleaner (mother-henning a covey of attachments) moved in; and finally the vases and valises we never use moved in there.

Being where it is, near the top of the T formed by the addition, my catchall Shangri-La serves as a corridor from dormitory to kitchen, unless the tribe troops through the bathroom detour. But since there's usually someone in the bathroom, all traffic flows by my desk. And if you're asking why I don't use my head and lock the door, it's because there is no door: some things had to go when the costs were mounting, and the door was one of them.

Because of the mass invasion, I'm exposed to a great deal of simple knowledge I either didn't get at their age or completely forgot. I pick it up mostly because I can't answer a lot of questions the school-agers fling at me. I shouldn't say I can't answer, because I seem to have a talent for what you might call the half answer. Apparently I know a little bit about a lot of things, but not a heck of a lot about anything except spelling, French, and history, none of which makes me a hero with the children. My knowledge of spelling does them little good, because I got it from looking up words and writing them out, and I insist that they do the same. My knowledge of French hasn't scored with them, because we're a long way from Montreal, and it isn't on their curriculum yet. And they've acquired precious little from my knowledge of history, because it's all Canadian, and there isn't much of a market for that in American schools.

But during homework hours they'll ask me what makes a geyser spout, and I have the half answer—because the water's boiling underground. But I can't explain what makes the water boil (can you?).

If they ask what Galileo was famous for I come up triumphantly with the telescope, but that's even worse than the half answer, because next day they inform me that Galileo also established the principle of the pendulum, discovered Jupiter and Saturn, and invented the barometer and air thermometer. It's embarrassing to have to trade homework answers with the neighbors. ("You tell me why leaves change color in the fall, and I'll tell you how a linotype works.") Why isn't anybody at school curious about Champlain, who founded Quebec? Or La Vérendrye, the explorer? Or General Montcalm, who almost defeated the British on the Plains of Abraham? I have a nagging dread that the kids will grow up with the vague idea that Canada is a massive, dormant chunk of latitude up there, populated by mounted police, *coureurs de bois*, tuqued lumberjacks (all named Pierre), buffalo, and quintuplets.

But that was the risk Helen and I knew we'd have to live with that November morning in the federal courtroom in Chicago when, with nervous pride, we raised our right hands and spoke the oath of citizenship. Because of what it meant to us, and because the Fifth Amendment is today so loosely pleaded, I'm setting it down here for Americans who have had no occasion to hear or read it.

"I hereby declare, on oath, that I absolutely and entirely renounce and abjure all allegiance and fidelity to any foreign prince, potentate, state or sovereignty, of whom or of which I have heretofore been a subject or citizen; that I will support and defend the Constitution and laws of the United States against all enemies, foreign and domestic; that I will bear true faith and allegiance to the same; that I will bear arms on behalf of the United States when required by the law; or that I will perform work of national importance under civilian direction when required by the law; and that I take this obligation freely, without any mental reservation or purpose of evasion—so help me God."

One night after dinner we settled down to a typical domestic scene. Helen was making the school lunches; Paul was fighting algebra; Georgia was washing the dishes; Shonagh was drying them; Nelda was running her bath water; Marcia was sweeping the floor; Lisa was scraping the day's mud off her shoes; Barbara was nearby, gobbling it up; and Mark sat in his high chair, wondering why dinner couldn't just go on and on.

"Do you know what day this is?" I asked the bustling brood.

"Easter!" cried Lisa, who'd been waiting for Easter since the day after Christmas.

"It's Shrove Tuesday," I said. There was no response, so I went on, "Shrove Tuesday means that tomorrow is Ash Wednesday."

"When's chocolate sundae?" persisted Lisa, ever the practical one.

"This means," I continued, "that Lent is here. What are you giving up for Lent?"

"I'm going to give up swimming," said Marcia, gazing idly out the window at a snowdrift.

"I won't fight with Jackie any more," chirped Lisa. (Jackie, her long-time neighbor pal, had moved away a month earlier.)

"I'm going to stop sucking my thumb," said Barbara, suddenly discovering that mud was more fun.

"My sacrifice," volunteered Nelda, who can't stand the cold, "will be to stay in the house and help Mother."

As usual, Paul, Georgia, and Shonagh announced that they were giving up candy, gum, and movies. But since the movie industry doesn't turn out much decent family film any more, we seldom let them go to the theater, and I reminded them that passing up the movies wouldn't constitute great heroics. So after long, deep thought, they decided to give up daytime television.

I must say that, by Eastertime, those three youngsters deserved a nice, comfortable halo. Not for the grace and goodness that come from self-discipline, but for the calm and repose they brought Helen and me. Seldom had the house been such a pleasant, peaceful place—not once in those forty days were we exposed to the simpering idiocies of daytime quiz games. Not once in those forty days did we have to wince at the savage imbecility of The Three Stooges. Silent was the inane laugh track of paid bubbleheads watching mediocre situation comedy. Gone was the Lone Ranger and that misfit Indian chum of his. Gone was Superman crashing through concrete in his tight long underwear, and gone were the freaks and monstrosities of ancient cartoons.

It was such a wonderfully tranquil Lent, I did more writing at home in those forty days than I did at the office. But Lent comes only once a year, and there are times when the study is simply too cramped and boisterous for serious work. One spring, involved in a major writing task, I decided to spend my vacation at the typewriter but away from the distractions at home. Passing by the school one morning, I had a brilliant impulse, and took it to the Reverend Joan Clare, whose Sister Superior mien doesn't quite conceal her angelic disposition. Would she let me use the auditorium in the school basement for three weeks for a good cause—earning extra money so I could pay what we owed on bus, milk, and tuition fees? (Sister Joan Clare never sends me dun letters; she just winks meaningly when we cross paths in the church vestibule Sunday mornings.)

Yes, Sister Superior thought, I could use the auditorium if I promised to watch myself with those awful cigarettes.

I got no work done the first day because I had to get the feel of the new surroundings, and there was much to explore—the jukebox and piano in the corner, the Coke machine, the bulletin board, and so on. And there were the quaint sounds from upstairs to get accustomed to—the hum of the water fountain, bells, foot patterings along the hall, bells, an occasional slamming door, bells, and group recitation from Grade One. ("*Thee* cat is in *thee* yard. Did *you* see *thee* cat? *Thee* dog runs *af*ter *thee* cat.")

On the second day I was determined to settle down, because now I was familiar with all the sights and sounds and smells. But in the morning, one of the women's groups convened on one side of the hall to plan an upcoming picnic, and I became terribly intrigued with a lengthy discussion on the relative merits of hamburger and wieners, how many cups should *really* be expected from a pound of coffee, and who was going to take charge of the potato salad. The afternoon booking was a rehearsal of Cub Scouts and Brownies for some ceremony, complete with presentation of colors, marching piano tunes, and plenty of hup-one-two-hup.

By Wednesday my daughters had spread the word that the man in the basement staring sadly at the typewriter was their father. I noticed that more and more little girls were trotting downstairs to the little girls' room, which was to the left of my niche, and more and more little boys were strolling to the little boys' room, which was to my right. By Thursday they were less nervous about it, and no longer needed bathroom excuses; they just stood in clusters at the doorway and stared and whispered and giggled, and during recess they were on their knees at the basement windows outside—them peering at me and me peering at them.

I had fled the house to escape the four little ones, and here I was—hopelessly surrounded by four hundred big ones. That weekend I told my troubles to Father Henehan, and on Monday morning I was installed in the basement of the church next door. There were no children here, and I was quite alone, except for God and an extremely suspicious janitor who, because of a language barrier, couldn't figure out who I was and what I was up to.

It happens that when I'm writing I like to rise every few minutes and pace the floor, a luxury that caused so many collisions at home, it had to be abandoned. But in the church cellar I had plenty of pacing room, and I took advantage of it. The difficulty was that the janitor felt it his duty to look in on me about every ten minutes, and each time he did, I'd be stalking up and down, gesturing and mumbling to myself like some ham actor learning a role. Complicating all this were the pilgrimages to a pew upstairs which I'd make each time I drew a blank. The stillness of the sanctuary struck me as ideal for inspiration, but commuting between basement and altar, unfortunately, left the frazzled janitor with the wretched picture of a man prowling downstairs and praying upstairs. I knew what was going through his mind: I was probably a defrocked priest trying to find himself again. Or perhaps a miserable sinner saddled with some unspeakable penance. Or maybe a spy from another denomination.

The fact that he was disturbed about it disturbed me, and as the week raced by, I found myself too distracted to work. Eventually it dawned on me that the peace and quiet were getting on my nerves, and by the third week I was back in the noisy, crowded study and the typewriter was clacking happily again.

I wasn't rejecting him, but for weeks after Mark was born I was disappointed that the last one hadn't been another girl. The distress always came on me when I was changing his diaper, because when you've had six girls in succession it's easy to forget your signals with that pin in your mouth. With little girls it isn't necessary to duck your head if they forget their manners when you're changing them. But after all those confident, dry years a male comes along and you keep forgetting that you have to be alert with boy babies, and you get your spirits dampened.

I mention this little annoyance because it helps to answer the question most often asked of parents of large families: "Don't you have an awful lot of problems?" What you have, really, is a few problems often. I caught it in the eye when Paul was in diapers, and I was catching it in the eye again (the same eye, for goodness' sake) a dozen years later, with Mark. Basically, the problems of child rearing are standard, almost identical, in a large family, with not too much variation in the areas of discipline and obedience. "Do as you're told!" sounds about the same when you say it to a two-year-old as when you say it to a six-year-old and to a ten-year-old, and generally the effects are not too diverse.

But there is little similarity of duplication in the blessings and compensations of having more children than you sometimes think you can handle. "I love you, Mommy," never sounds the same—it's a different, ever-changing thing from child to child, and it remains distinctly novel from the same child the hundredth time around. And after a long time, when you think you know the taste and the touch and the warmth of a child's kiss, the child kisses you once more for the thousandth time, and you find it's new and original all over again.

(There was a tiresome sameness about our last Halloween —I began to wonder if I could face another, with the carving of a pumpkin head with eight helpers, creating costumes from old clothes, the freezing waits outside while the toddlers trick-or-treated from door to door. But when at night's end they decided among themselves to take half their loot to an orphanage, this again was part of the continuing newness.)

After the eighth baby came I decided to resign myself to the fact that we would never be rich. But what is wealth, really?

There's a sort of accidental symbol of all this in a picture of Helen and me that hangs on a wall in the study. When people show an interest in it, I play a little game I made up: I ask them if they see anything unusual about the picture. Since we're wearing wild grins and I'm holding a highball, they invariably remark that we seem to be having a ball, laughing it up.

The picture was taken five years ago at a benefit featuring the Harry Winston jewel collection. Dangling from Helen's neck is the extravagant Hope diamond, but in the photo the legendary gem looks no more impressive than Helen's fifty-cent earrings. And all that people notice is that we're laughing it up. I look at that print often, because it's a picture of happiness, and I gaze at the world's best-known pendant (valued in excess of a million dollars) and then at Helen's fifty-cent earrings, and it tells me quite a story about the difference between wealth and happiness.

Because there are compensations for not being rich. Since we can't afford to climb aboard the carrousel that spins around the giddy world of feverish self-indulgence, we turn to each other for the pleasures some seek in vain with money. To hear a child say he can't wait until Saturday "because then you'll be home all day" is something that can't be bought—not with ten times ten Hope diamonds.

There is truth in the saying that the hungry fighter makes the best fighter. Recently I won the Festival of Leadership Award as Chicago's Outstanding Journalist, but I know very well that this good fortune wouldn't have come to me if I didn't have Helen and that mob at home to work for and live with.

Not rich? When we've been singled out by God to take nine of His images—even though He took one, Patricia, back.

Not rich? When I'm joined for life to a girl whose face and figure turn my spine to jelly as they did the night when I first saw her exciting reflection in the mirror?

Not rich? I head the world's most opulent corporation, because there isn't a dividend around that matches the fun of being in love with Helen, and romanced by eight prejudiced kids.

But I do have one regret—the time, the precious time of being with them, is so brief and fleeting. I wish the breakfasts were longer. I wish we could be together at midday. And I wish the dark goodnights wouldn't come so soon in the evening. That's why I saw possibilities in the toy suggestion box I received in the publicity mail one day. I took it home, tacked it to the kitchen wall, and waited for a barrage of family communication.

The next morning I opened the box. It contained only one suggestion. It was from Helen.

All it said was: "Eight is enough."